COPPER

CATTLE

COTTON

Printed in the United States of America by
Taylor Specialty Books, Commercial Division of Balfour/Taylor
www.taylorspecialtybooks.com

Published by:

MMPR
MARKETING

*This book is dedicated to the servers,
bussers and dishwashers, for without you
we would have missing ingredients!*

100

100 YEARS
100 CHEFS
100 RECIPES

A CULINARY TRIBUTE
CELEBRATING
ARIZONA'S CENTENNIAL

1912-2012

CONTRIBUTING WRITERS:

NIKKI BUCHANAN

MICHELE LAUDIG

MMPR MARKETING

TABLE OF CONTENTS

LETTER FROM THE PUBLISHER

How to begin a love letter to Arizona...

Arizona has been, and always will be, my home. In a very short amount of time, the great state of Arizona has blossomed from a Wild West frontier to a well-groomed, culturally rich tourist destination backboned by one of the great wonders of the world, the Grand Canyon. Modern pioneers have continued to push the limits, creating national events such as The Waste Management Phoenix Open, The Arabian Horse Show, the largest classic car shows in the southwest, and the Scottsdale Culinary Festival that now thrive in our world-class climate. Visitors and locals alike delight in the diversity of our landscape, from cactus-covered deserts to pine trees and snow-capped mountains—just an hour apart.

It's no surprise that tourism is a driving force in the Grand Canyon State. More than 30 million people visit each year, and an increasing number are coming in droves to explore our culinary scene. Sure, Arizona's economy is traditionally backed by the five C's—Copper, Climate, Citrus, Cattle and Cotton—but there really should be a sixth C—Culinary. Some of the greatest leaders of the past century have wielded a chef's knife, a pan and a vision, so as we approach Arizona's 100th birthday, we have an opportunity to recognize the wealth of our culinary prowess.

From famous James Beard chefs to grassroots eateries, the chefs in this book have helped to shape the way people taste in the Southwest. As you can imagine, it was extremely difficult selecting the 100 dining destinations that make up a snapshot of our scene, but we took the approach of highlighting restaurants—some historic and some new, but all are important in their own way. They symbolize trends, staples, the classics and the fusion. Some have tapped into locally grown food from meat and cheeses to veggies and citrus, while others have brought their experiences abroad back to within our borders.

Move over LA, Chicago and New York. Step aside San Francisco. We may never have a walking city, but come drive with us though the places that will warm your heart, and discover what we've been talking about for a long time.

Margo Kesler

ARIZONA: A SPECTACULAR LAND OF ANOMALIES AND TAMALES

By Marshall Trimble, Official Arizona State Historian

As we celebrate our 100th birthday we remember that Arizona is a place that lives by its myths, legends, contrasts and, especially, its contradictions. For example, the first white man to come to Arizona was a black man; the first native Arizona cowboy movie star was a cowgirl; the Lost Dutchman was a German, and the gunfight at OK Corral didn't occur at the OK Corral. New York Mayor Fiorello La Guardia, grew up in Prescott; and back around 1900, the largest family living in Strawberry was named Peach.

Foodwise, there are many examples. Take for instance that Tombstone, known as The Town Too Tough To Die, was considered by Easterners a rough-and-tumble place that served nothing but coffee, beef and beans. But, in fact, not only could you order fine wines and oysters under glass, the Occidental Hotel Sunday dinner menu entrees included "Pinonsa Poulett aux Champignons, Cream Fricassee of Chicken, Asparagus Points, Casserole d'Ritz au Oeufs al Chinois; and Ducks of Mutton, braze, with Chipoluta Ragout." All entrees were served for fifty cents.

Then there was Jim Sam, who operated restaurants serving Chinese cuisine in a number of mining towns including Pinal City. One day a local undesirable named Shoot 'Em Up Dick came in and ordered the most expensive dish on the menu. After finishing he ordered a fancy cigar, lit it and got up to leave.

"Hey, you forgot something," Jim Sam said.

"No, I didn't forget nothin'. I am Shoot 'Em Up Dick."

Jim Sam, who was also known as a good man with a meat cleaver, grabbed a big pistol and said, "So, you Shoot 'Em Up Dick? I am Shoot 'Em Down Jim Sam. You pay up plenty quick."

Shoot 'Em Up Dick paid up pronto.

In other food lore, a Greek immigrant named Louis Shepard was managing the Window Rock Lodge in Apache County. Working late one night in 1963, he decided to have a midnight snack but didn't want to dirty a plate so he made one out of a slab of fry bread, poured some beans on it and — a regional favorite, the Navajo taco, was born.

The state is famous for its Mexican food and a large group of Arizonans want to make the chimichanga the "Official Food of Arizona." A chimichanga is a burrito prepared with a choice of meat, vegetables and spices then deep-fried. Salsa, guacamole and sour cream often top the dish. Restaurants in both Phoenix and Tucson claim bragging rights. The strongest claim comes from the El Charro Cafe, the oldest Mexican restaurant in Tucson, where the residents boldly proclaim the Old Pueblo the "Mexican Food Capital of the U.S."

Family legend says Monica Flin, who started the restaurant in 1922, accidentally flipped a pastry into the deep fryer. She was about to say a cuss word, but noticed her young nieces and nephews were in the kitchen with her so she quickly changed the swear word to "chimichanga," the Spanish equivalent of "thingamagig." And that name stuck.

Arizona history offers many great anomalies—and its fine and humble, old and new restaurants offer lots of good eating!

Marshall Trimble has written more than 25 books about Arizona and co-authored several others. He has received many honors as a historian, writer and performer, including the governor appointing him the Official State Historian in 1997.

In preparation for the state's 100th anniversary, he was appointed by the governor to the Arizona Centennial Commission. He was also a member of the Governor's Commission in 1987 celebrating the state's 75th Anniversary.

A native Arizonan, Trimble was born in Mesa and grew up in Ash Fork, a small railroad town along old Route 66. He makes his home in Scottsdale.

610 E. 8th St., Tempe, Arizona, 1912.

RECIPES

100

BELGIAN DARK CHOCOLATE TART

Recipe courtesy of
Amuse Bouche
Chef Kierstin Mor
Phoenix
623-322-8881

SERVES 6

BUTTER SHORT CRUST

1 stick + 1 tablespoon	unsalted butter for brushing
1 3/4 cups	all-purpose unbleached flour
1 teaspoon	salt
1 tablespoon	granulated sugar
1	egg yolk
1/4 cup	ice cold water

CHOCOLATE FILLING

16 ounces	dark chocolate (60-65 percent cocoa)
2 cups	heavy whipping cream
4	egg yolks
	Pinch of salt

11

1. Preheat oven to 375 degrees. Place butter, flour, salt and sugar in a bowl of a food processor. In a separate bowl, mix egg yolk and water.

2. Start food processor and mix until the butter is fully incorporated into flour. The mixture's texture will resemble rough sand. While food processor is still running, pour wet mix into flour mix and continue mixing until dough forms into a ball. Be careful not to overmix or the dough will turn tough.

3. Wrap dough tightly in plastic wrap and refrigerate for at least 2 hours or overnight. Take dough out and let sit until softened and can easily be pressed with a thumb. Brush tart mold with 1 tablespoon butter.

4. On a well-floured surface, flatten the dough with a rolling pin and line it in the tart mold and cut off excess dough. Place tart shell in the freezer until fully frozen.

5. Preheat oven to 375 degrees. Line bottom and sides of tart shell with plastic wrap and fill with pie weights or dried beans. Bake for 15 minutes or until the edges are brown. Remove the wrap and beans. Turn off oven and allow tart shell to bake 10 additional minutes to dry out.

6. To prepare the chocolate filling, lower oven to 225 degrees. Bring cream to a boil with a pinch of salt. Place chocolate in mixing bowl and pour cream over chocolate. Whisk together until the chocolate is fully melted. While whisking, add egg yolks one by one until fully combined.

7. Pour chocolate mixture into baked tart shell and bake in 225-degree oven for 15 minutes. Allow tart to cool in the refrigerator for at least 2 hours. Slice and serve with vanilla whipped cream, vanilla ice cream or fresh berries. The tart is best served the day it is made, but it will keep for three days in your fridge covered with a plastic wrap.

In the literal translation from French, Amuse Bouche means "entertains the mouth," and in Phoenix, entertaining the palate is what Amuse Bouche does best. Whether you are dining-in at the bistro, surrounded by deep-red walls, or having its catering team come to you, the food will captivate your senses and heart. The lunch, dinner and Sunday breakfast menus are filled with unique and alluring fare that takes traditional dishes and infuses them with an unforgettable French and Southwestern flair.

ROASTED BUTTERNUT SQUASH SOUP

Recipe courtesy of
The Asylum
Chef Richard D. Pasich
Jerome
928-639-3197

Seventy years after Phelps Dodge built a '20s-era, state-of-the-art hospital for its copper miners on Cleopatra Hill, the gracious old building (rumored to have ghosts) was converted into the Jerome Grand Hotel. In 2001, the hotel's multi-windowed, second floor restaurant became The Asylum, which features spectacular 75-mile views of the Verde Valley, an award-winning wine list and a menu that nicely straddles the fence between upscale and casual. Chef-owners Rich Pasich and Jen Nagel are famous for their butternut squash soup, sparked with local Oak Creek Amber Ale. You might say its flavor is haunting.

SERVES 6

2	large whole butternut squash, roasted
2	poblano peppers, roasted and peeled
1	white onion, chopped
3/4 cup	Oak Creek Amber beer (or favorite amber)
2 cups	chicken stock
1/2 cup	brown sugar
1 tablespoon	garlic, minced
1 pinch	cinnamon
1 pinch	nutmeg
1	serrano chile, finely minced
1 cup	heavy cream
	Salt and pepper to taste
1 bunch	green onions

CREMA

1/2 cup	heavy cream
	Juice of 1 lime
	Pinch of cinnamon

1. Preheat oven to 400 degrees. Cut the squash in half, remove seeds. Place in shallow roasting pan filled with an inch of water and roast for 45 minutes or until very tender. Remove from oven and cool.

2. To roast chiles, cut in half and remove seeds. Place on flat baking sheet in 400 degree oven and roast about 15 minutes, or until skin begins to blacken. Remove from oven and place in a sealable bag for about 5 minutes. Remove and peel. Heat a skillet on high heat until scorching hot. Sauté onions and chiles, stirring constantly, for a few minutes. Add beer and scrape onion and pepper bits from bottom of the pan. Add chicken stock, peeled squash, and remaining ingredients except for cream, onions, lime and cinnamon. Reduce heat and simmer for 30 minutes. Remove and carefully pour into a food processor or blender. Puree. Remove pot from heat and add puree to pot. Fold in cream. Salt and pepper to taste. Chop green onions and garnish.

3. In a separate bowl, mix heavy cream, lime juice and cinnamon. Whip until the cream becomes thick. Place in sandwich bag. Cut a small corner tip of bottom off for impromptu pastry bag and garnish squash puree with a dollop.

SMOKED SALMON
WITH A TATER TOT AND SHAVED FENNEL

Recipe courtesy of
Atlas Bistro
Chef Joshua Riesner and
Chef Keenan Bosworth
Scottsdale
480-990-2433

SERVES 4

1 side	salmon, bloodline and skin removed
1	fennel bulb
1	grapefruit
1	lemon
1	lime
1	orange
1 tablespoon	toasted coriander seeds
1 tablespoon	toasted fennel seeds
2 cups	white sugar
2 cups	Kosher salt
	Fennel fronds and lemon juice for garnishing

TATER TOTS

2 cups	mashed potatoes
	Flour for dusting
2	eggs, beaten
1 cup	panko breadcrumbs
	Canola oil for frying

1. Chop the fennel and citrus, discarding rind, into 1-inch cubes. Place in a food processor with the toasted seeds and puree until juicy and soft. Pour into a non-aluminum pan large enough to hold the fish and stir in the salt and sugar.

2. Add the salmon and rub the mixture on it until it is completely covered. Make sure to get more of the salt mix on top before covering the pan with plastic. Place in the refrigerator for at least 16 hours. The fish is cured when the thin tails are somewhat hard, and the middles are firm to touch. Do not marinate too long or else the fish will lose its creamy texture. Rinse the salmon under cold running water to stop the curing process. Remove any citrus seeds. Ignite a few pieces of charcoal under a grill, cook until they smolder, and add hot apple wood chips. Add salmon on rack above coal and wood chips. Place a tray of ice below the rack to keep temperatures from becoming too hot. Allow fish to smoke until smoke disappears, about 1 hour. Check periodically to make sure there is no fire and that the smoke does not prematurely burn out.

3. To make tater tots, scoop 1 heaping tablespoon mashed potatoes. Roll into a ball and dust with flour. Dip in egg wash, completely coating the potato ball. Next, roll in panko breadcrumbs. Set aside. Repeat for remaining potatoes. Heat a large sauté pan on medium high heat. Fill with about 1/2 inch canola oil. When hot, add several potato balls and fry until golden brown, about 5-7 minutes, turning occasionally to brown all sides. Use a slotted spoon to remove. Set aside and keep warm while frying the remaining batches.

4. To serve, place the potato tots on a large serving platter. Stack thinly sliced salmon on top. Top with fennel fronds and lemon juice.

An intimate fine-dining restaurant tucked discreetly into a strip mall, Atlas Bistro is one of Scottsdale's hidden gems. While it may be hard to spot, food and wine connoisseurs have honed in on it as the city's best BYOB, a place where exceptional contemporary American cuisine is crafted especially to complement wines. Forgot your bottle? No problem. Guests have to enter the dining room through AZ Wine Company, which is right next door. Chefs Joshua Riesner and Keenan Bosworth say they're proud to share their smoked salmon recipe, an excellent all-weather dish that's great for entertaining groups because of its surprising ease of preparation. It's one of the longest-standing and best-selling dishes on the menu at Atlas, which opened in 2004.

OSSOBUCO MILANESE

Recipe courtesy of
Avanti
Chef Angiolo Livi
Phoenix
602-956-0900

Cozy booths wrapped in graphic zebra print, mirrored ceilings, and dim lighting create an intimate atmosphere for enjoying old-school Italian cuisine and a globe-trotting selection of wines at this longstanding Phoenix favorite. Chef Angiolo Livi (an Italian immigrant – and an Arizona Culinary Hall of Fame-award winner) caters to a loyal, well-heeled clientele. Romance is in the air here, for sure, but there's just as much seduction on the plate. In fact, his ossobuco has been on the menu since 1974 and remains the most-requested dish by customers. Considering how much Avanti raised the bar for sophisticated international dining when it first came onto the scene, this recipe could well be considered one of Livi's finest contributions to Arizona culinary history.

SERVES 6

6	veal shanks
3/4 cup	all-purpose flour for dredging
	Salt and freshly ground pepper to taste
14 tablespoons	olive oil, divided
2	medium white onions
1	garlic clove
2	shallots
7	peeled carrots
1	celery rib
1	celery stalk
1/2 teaspoon	thyme
1 teaspoon	fresh tarragon
2	bay leaves
1/4 cup	chopped fresh parsley
1 cup	dry white wine
3 cups	chicken stock
15 ounces	peeled, deseeded tomatoes (juice included) (about 5-6 tomatoes)

1. Preheat oven to 375 degrees. Season flour with salt and pepper. Dunk veal shanks in flour and shake off excess. Set aside. In a large, heavy pan, heat 6 tablespoons olive oil until very hot. Sear the veal shanks in the hot oil. Turn them over, browning, but not burning, each side evenly. Set aside.

2. Finely chop onion, garlic and shallots. Slice carrots in 1/4 inch circles. Slice celery in 1/4 inch half-moon. Add remaining 4 ounces of olive oil in a large roasting pan on medium heat. Sauté onions, garlic and shallots, about 5-7 minutes, or until onions and celery are transparent. Add thyme, tarragon, bay leaves and chopped parsley.

3. Place the browned veal shanks over the vegetables. Pour the dry white wine and 1/2 of the chicken stock over the veal shanks. On high, boil uncovered until liquid has reduced by one third. While shanks and liquid are cooking, prepare approximately 5-6 tomatoes by blanching, peeling and deseeding them. To blanch tomatoes, drop them in boiling water for about 15 seconds, then remove, and drop immediately into cold water. Then chop coarsely when cool and retain juices.

4. When liquid has reduced by a third, add tomatoes, the remaining chicken stock and salt and pepper. Cover the pan and place in oven for 1 1/2 -2 hours. Check on liquid in pan periodically. If liquid has reduced too much, add more chicken stock and about 1/3 cup white wine. When done, veal shanks should be extremely tender, and the sauce glossy and thick.

CHILES EN NOGADA

SERVES 4

4	poblano peppers, roasted and peeled
2	chicken breasts
1 tablespoon	olive oil
2 teaspoon	diced onion
1	clove garlic, minced
1 teaspoon	apricots, dried
1 teaspoon	apples, diced
1 teaspoon	pears
1 teaspoon	raisins
1 teaspoon	craisins
2 teaspoon	tomato paste
1 cup	white wine
	Sugar, salt and pepper, to taste
	Cilantro and pomegranate seeds for garnish, optional

CREAM SAUCE

1	shallot, minced
1	clove garlic, minced
1 cup	white wine
2 cups	heavy cream
1/4 cup	almonds, ground
	Salt and pepper, to taste

Recipe courtesy of
Barrio Café
Chef Silvana Salcido Esparza
Phoenix
602-636-0240

"I really love how Arizona is a place where anything is possible," says Chef Silvana Salcido Esparza. "I came to Arizona with nothing but a desire to become a chef and a suitcase full of my grandmother's recipes."

In 2002, her dream came true when she and partner Wendy Gruber founded Barrio Cafe, setting the bar for refined regional Mexican food in the Valley of the Sun. Her Chiles en Nogada is a specialty of central Mexico and is served at the restaurant from September until April. "The red, white and green entrée is as traditional as the Mexican flag, while the dried-fruit stuffing and almond garnish illustrate the bold interpretation that I bring to all my food," she explains. "This award-winning seasonal dish is a favorite of my clients. I enjoy knowing that they can experience the pleasure of cooking it in their own homes."

1. Preheat oven to 375 degrees. Cut poblano peppers in half, remove seeds and lightly coat with olive oil. Place peppers cut side down on roasting sheet. Roast 15-20 minutes, or until peppers begin to blister and turn black in spots. Remove and place in a sealable bag to sweat for about 10 minutes. Remove and peel. Set aside.

2. Next, dice the chicken breasts into bite-size pieces. In a hot sauté pan, add oil and, when hot, add diced chicken breast and sauté until chicken starts to turn white, about 2-3 minutes. Add diced onions and continue to sauté until onions are translucent, about 3-5 minutes. Add chopped garlic, apricots and remaining fresh and dried fruit. Sauté for 1 minute. Add paste and continue to sauté until paste has covered all of the ingredients. Add white wine and continue to cook until chicken is tender, about 1-2 minutes. Season to taste.

3. Allow peppers to cool slightly, then stuff with equal amounts of chicken-fruit mix. Keep warm while making sauce.

4. To make sauce, add oil and shallots to a sauté pan, and cook until shallots are translucent, about 5-7 minutes. At this point, add garlic and continue to sauté until garlic has turned light caramel. Add wine and reduce until almost gone. Add heavy cream and reduce by half in volume. Adjust seasoning and finish with almonds.

5. Pour sauce over peppers and garnish with cilantro and pomegranate seeds.

FIG AND PECAN PIE
WITH CITRUS CREAM CHEESE ICE CREAM

Recipe courtesy of
Beckett's Table
Chef Justin Beckett
Phoenix
602-954-1700

SERVES 8

PIE DOUGH

3/4 cup	sugar
1 pound	soft butter
2 1/2 cups	all-purpose flour (pasta flour)
4 ounces	cornstarch
1 cup, plus	toasted and chopped pecans

PECAN PIE FILLING

1 cup	sugar
1/2 cup	light corn syrup
1/4 cup	melted butter
3	eggs
1 cup	toasted and chopped pecans
2 tablespoons	chopped figs

CITRUS ZEST CREAM CHEESE ICE CREAM

1 cup	cream cheese
1/2 cup	sour cream
1/2 cup	heavy cream
3/4 cup	sugar
1/2	lemon zest and juice
1/2	orange zest and juice
1 teaspoon	vanilla

1. To make pecan pie dough, add sugar and butter to a mixing bowl and cream or blend well together. Add flour, cornstarch and nuts. Stir until completely blended. Divide dough in half and wrap tightly in plastic. Refrigerate for at least 1 hour before rolling out into pie shell. Before rolling, dust clean surface with flour to prevent sticking. Roll into a circle big enough for a pie pan. Keep refrigerated while preparing filling.

2. To make pie filling, preheat oven to 400 degrees and combine all ingredients. Pour into chilled pie shell. Bake for 10 minutes. Turn down oven to 350 degrees and bake for 35 minutes or until pie does not jiggle.

3. For the ice cream, combine all ingredients into food processor and spin till smooth. Place into an ice cream spinner and spin till frozen. To serve, cut the pie into 8 pieces and serve with a large scoop of ice cream.

Walk through the doors of Beckett's Table and you will find yourself transported to an alehouse lodge, with wooden rafters pushing down the aromas from the open kitchen environment into the collective dining space. Chef Justin Beckett is constantly perusing the local farmers markets for seasonal inspiration, a focal point on his menu which features Seared Salmon with Roasted Cauliflower, Golden Raisins and Fennel Puree, as well as comfort food favorites such as Beef Bourguignon Shepherd's Pie with mashed potatoes, tender beef, veggies.

HALIBUT EN PAPILLOTE

Recipe courtesy of
Binkley's
Chef Kevin Binkley
Cave Creek
480-437-1072

Photo: David Zickl

SERVES 2-4

4	sweet onions
2 tablespoons	canola oil
8 sprigs	Italian parsley
8 sprigs	thyme
3 quarts	chicken stock
4	cippolini onions, cut into quarters
4	baby carrots, white, orange, yellow and red, peeled and sliced into rounds
2	baby turnips, cut into quarters
1/4 head	savoy cabbage
2 pieces	about 6 ounces each, of halibut
1 cup	cooked rice beans
2 tablespoons	unsalted butter
	Kosher salt, white pepper to taste
2 pieces	Fata paper
2 pieces	butcher's twine, cut 1 foot long

Whether they trek to Cave Creek from Downtown Phoenix or fly across a few time zones, food fanatics inevitably seek out this elegant, unpretentious spot for an exceptional experience rather than simply a good meal. Chef Kevin Binkley, who cooked at The French Laundry and The Inn at Little Washington before opening his restaurant in 2004 with his wife, Amy, has been praised by Bon Appetit *and* Food + Wine *for his inventive tasting menus. Working closely with local farmers as much as possible to source pristine ingredients, he takes pride in serving the best of Arizona's bounty, as exemplified by the list of fresh vegetables used in this halibut recipe.*

1. Preheat oven to 285 degrees. Split onions and toss with canola oil and salt. Place in a pan and cover with parsley and thyme. Wrap with foil and put in oven. Cook for approximately 3 hours, until very tender and juice is released from the onions.

2. Pour contents of roasting pan and pour into a stock pot. Cover with chicken stock. Bring to a low simmer and cook slowly for 2 hours. Strain through a fine mesh sieve. Season with salt.

3. While the pot simmers, in a separate pan cook carrots, cippolini and turnips in olive oil. Cool and reserve one cup liquid. Heat sauté pan on medium heat, add olive oil, and when hot, the vegetables. Sauté for about 10-15 minutes, or until vegetables are al dente and liquid released. Cool and reserve 1 cup liquid.

4. Julienne the cabbage and cover with 1/2 of the jus from the onions and simmer until tender, about 8-10 minutes. Cool and store in liquid.

5. To assemble: place Fata paper in a bowl. Remove cabbage from liquid and place on Fata paper. Then add carrots, turnips and cippolini onion. Add approximately 3/4 cup of the reserved onion jus. Season the halibut with salt and white pepper and place on top of vegetables. Place 1 tablespoon of butter on top of each fish. Pull Fata paper up and around fish and tie tight at top to seal with butcher's twine.

6. To cook: place Fata paper wrapped fish in a small cast iron skillet and slowly heat until liquid simmers in bag. It should only take 3-4 minutes to cook. Do not remove from skillet, and serve while still simmering. Cut top of bag, just below butcher's twine, and open bag.

GRILLED SHRIMP
WITH CHIMICHURRI

If you've been in the Valley of the Sun long enough, you remember Bobby McGee's. Created in 1971 by the legendary Bob Sikora, the concept soon became a franchise. Thirty-five years later, Sikora sold the franchise but retained the original Bobby McGee's location. For his next concept, he scoured the United States in pursuit of quintessential barbecue flavors and techniques. Using this knowledge, Bob created Bobby Q's and serves up smoky brisket, chicken, steaks and ribs that fall to pieces into flavor-packed morsels. Thank "Q," Bob, for your contribution.

SERVES 4

2 pounds	large shrimp (21 to 25 count)
1 cup	olive oil, divided
	Pack of skewers, at least 20

CHIMICHURRI SAUCE

1 cup	chopped fresh parsley
3 tablespoons	chopped fresh garlic
1/4 teaspoon	crushed red pepper
1 teaspoon	Kosher salt
1 teaspoon	coarse black pepper

1. Prepare grill for cooking over medium-hot charcoal, medium heat for gas. Toss shrimp with 1 tablespoon oil, 1/4 teaspoon salt and 1/4 teaspoon pepper in a bowl. Next, thread 4 or 5 shrimp onto each skewer, careful not to crowd shrimp to allow for even cooking.

2. To make the Chimichurri Sauce, add parsley, garlic, red pepper, salt and pepper to a blender. Blend until completely blended.

3. Lightly oil grill and add shrimp skewers. Grill about 2 minutes, turning and grilling another 2-3 minutes, basting frequently with Chimichurri Sauce.

Recipe courtesy of
Bobby Q's
Chef Mark Hittle
Phoenix
602-995-5982

PAN-ROASTED RIDGEVIEW FARMS CHICKEN WITH GRILLED SQUASH
AND RED POTATOES IN A CHEVRE VINAIGRETTE AND BASIL PESTO

Recipe courtesy of
Brix Restaurant & Wine Bar
Chef David Smith
Flagstaff
928-774-0541

Brix, the wine term for the sugar-content of grapes at harvest, is the fitting name of Paul and Laura Moir's snug farm-focused restaurant housed in a 1909 brick building, specializing in seasonal American cooking and, of course, great wine. The structure was originally a garage for wealthy banker T.E. Pollock, who owned the first car in Flagstaff. Now it's a romantic haven for diners who appreciate Moir's meticulous sourcing and Chef David Smith's culinary chops, both deliciously illustrated in this recipe using chickens and squash from the Verde Valley and goat cheese from Snowflake.

SERVES 4

1	medium zucchini
1	medium yellow summer squash
1/2	Japanese eggplant
	Olive oil for tossing
	Salt and pepper to taste
1/2 cup	Black Mesa Ranch chevre
1/4 cup	white wine vinegar
1	shallot, minced
1 teaspoon	fresh thyme
1	clove garlic, minced
1 cup	extra virgin olive oil
2 cups	packed fresh basil
1/2 cup	toasted pine nuts
2	cloves garlic, chopped
	Juice of 1 lemon
1/2 cup	shaved Parmigiano Reggiano
1/2 cup	toasted pine nuts
4	Ridgeview Farm boneless chicken breasts, skin on
1 tablespoon	butter
1 tablespoon	fresh chopped parsley
	Salt and pepper to taste

1. Slice the zucchini and squash into lengthwise planks. Slice the eggplant diagonally. Season eggplant with salt and place on a rack to cure for 10-15 minutes. Pat dry excess water with paper towels.

2. Then, toss the squash and zucchini with a little oil, salt and pepper. Heat grill to medium high heat, and when hot, grill vegetables, about 3-5 minutes a side, or until grill marks appear. Remove, dice and set to the side. Place the Chevre, vinegar, shallot, thyme and garlic in a blender. Mix on high while slowly adding the oil. Add water if necessary to thin mixture. Continue adding the oil until the vinaigrette emulsifies into a smooth, fluffy looking sauce. Season with salt and pepper. Set aside.

3. In a food processor, pulse basil, garlic, lemon and Parmigiano Reggiano, adding oil to suit your preference. Transfer from processor into mixing bowl.

4. Preheat oven to 350 degrees. Place pine nuts in an even layer on baking sheet. Bake for 6-10 minutes, stirring occasionally, until golden brown. Remove from oven. Fold pine nuts and Parmigiano Reggiano with a spatula into the processor. Salt and pepper to taste.

5. Increase temperature to 400 degrees. Over medium-high heat, lightly oil a cast iron pan and wait until the oil just starts to smoke. Season the chicken with salt and pepper. Lay the breast, skin side down, into the pan. Cook until skin is golden crisp, approximately 5 minutes. Turn the chicken over and place cast iron pan on center rack in the oven. Cook for 12 to 15 minutes or until the internal temperature reaches 165 degrees.

6. In a separate pan, add 1 tablespoon butter and the diced squash. Sauté on medium heat for 2 minutes, add eggplant and sauté for 1 minute. Add tablespoon of parsley at the end, salt and pepper to taste. Place the sautéed vegetable mixture into the center of the plate, cut the chicken in half and lay over vegetables, top with basil pesto and Chevre vinaigrette.

SMOKED BRISKET AND BLACK EYED PEA CHILI

Recipe courtesy of
Bryan's Black Mountain BBQ
Chef Bryan Dooley
Cave Creek
480-575-7155

SERVES 4-6

2 tablespoons	olive oil
3/4 cup	red onion, diced
3	garlic cloves, minced
3 tablespoons	chili powder
1 teaspoon	salt
1/4 teaspoon	black pepper
1 can (28 ounces)	whole, crushed tomatoes
1 can (15 ounces)	black-eyed peas, rinsed and drained
1 pound	brisket, roasted or smoked, chopped
1/2	jalapeño, chopped (optional)

1. Heat sauté pan on medium high. Add olive oil, and when hot add onion and garlic. Sauté, stirring frequently, until onion softens, about 5 minutes. Add chili powder, salt and pepper. Stir well.

2. Add canned tomatoes with their juice, black-eyed peas and chopped brisket. Reduce heat to simmer, cover and cook for 30 to 45 minutes to allow flavors to blend. Add chopped jalapeño before serving, if desired.

The illuminated, giant green cactus may catch your eye as you pull up to Bryan's Black Mountain BBQ, but that, my friend, is just the tip of this BBQ iceberg. What makes this barbecue joint stand out is Chef-owners Donna and Bryan Dooley's focus on the quality of their meat and the secret rub combo that Bryan considers the key to his barbecue kingdom. Just imagine a barbecue utopia filled with charred chickens, sliced beef brisket and juicy, tender slabs of pork ribs— and that's Bryan's Black Mountain BBQ.

MOLE DE CHILHUACLE

WITH SHREDDED CHICKEN

Recipe courtesy of
Café Poca Cosa
Chef Suzana Davila
Tucson
520-622-6400

Photo: Kristin April Photography

SERVES 8-10

8	chicken breasts
1	carrot
3	yellow onions
12	garlic cloves
	Salt and pepper to taste
1/2 cup	vegetable oil
4 cups	sesame seeds
2 cups	fresh almonds, shelled
1 cup	roasted peanuts, shelled
10	chilhuacle chilis
6	pasilla chilis
3	guajillo chilis
4	large Roma tomatoes
1 cup	red chili powder
3	cinnamon sticks
4	cloves
1 tablespoon	oregano
4 tablespoons	sugar
8-10 cups	chicken broth
	Tortillas, beans, and rice for serving

1. Clean chicken breasts and place them in a large pot with enough water to yield a gallon of chicken broth. The ingredients of the mole will absorb quite a bit of liquid. Cut up carrot, 1 onion and 1 clove garlic. Heat on medium high heat until water begins to simmer, but not boil. Cook simmering for about 20 minutes. Remove chicken breasts, and place on a plate to cool. Pull meat from bones, cover and reserve in the refrigerator.

2. In a large sauté pan, pour about half vegetable oil into a large sauté pan. Mix in sesame seeds, almonds and peanuts. Brown until golden, about 5 minutes. Remove and reserve nuts.

3. Heat grill on medium high heat. Lightly oil and add peppers, one onion cut into large slices, tomatoes and remaining garlic on a grill, turning until the skins of all are lightly charred, about 7-9 minutes. Remove vegetables, and in batches with nuts and seeds, add to a food processor and puree. Continue in batches.

4. In a large, dry sauté pan, cook the red chili powder with the cinnamon, cloves and oregano. Place the browned seasonings in holding dish. Take the remaining onion, cut it up, and place it in the large sauté pan with remaining oil. Slowly add the mixture from the food processor and the reserved seasonings.

5. Cook over medium heat for 20 minutes, adding chicken broth to create a loose but thick consistency. Add sugar and stir additional chicken broth into mixture. Add shredded chicken. Serve with tortillas, rice and Ranchero beans.

It's easy to get swept away by the Mexican mystique of Café Poca Cosa. Chef and owner Suzana Davila uses indigenous Mexican ingredients to recreate traditional dishes and craft inspired new flavors. The restaurant gives diners a one-of-a-kind experience, as the chalkboard menu changes twice daily. The cuisine is served in a modern, bistro-style dining room splashed with rich tomato-red walls that whisk you away on a culinary escapade unlike any other in Tucson.

HERB-ROASTED SWEET POTATOES
WITH ANAHEIM CHILES AND PECANS

Recipe courtesy of
Café ZuZu
Chef Chuck Wiley
Scottsdale
480-421-7997

Photo: Kristin April Photography

SERVES 4

2 pounds or about 5 cups	sweet potato, peeled and cut into 3/4" cubes
1	small red onion, cut into 3/4" dice
2 teaspoons	rosemary
2 cloves	garlic, chopped
1/2 teaspoon	coriander, freshly toasted and ground
1 tablespoon	olive oil
	Kosher salt and freshly ground black pepper to taste
1	large red bell pepper — roasted, peeled, and cut in strips
1-2	Anaheim chili — roasted, peeled, and cut in strips
2 teaspoons	white wine vinegar
1/4 cup	pecans, toasted
2 teaspoons	parsley, chopped

1. Preheat oven to 475 degrees. Place a large roasting pan in the oven and heat until very hot. Meanwhile, in a large mixing bowl, combine the sweet potato, onion, garlic, rosemary and coriander. Add the olive oil; season with salt and pepper and toss to coat.

2. Pour the sweet potato and onion into the hot roasting pan and stir. Place back in the oven and roast until potatoes are cooked through, stirring occasionally; about 25-30 minutes. To roast red pepper and chiles, cut in half and remove seeds. Lightly coat with olive oil and place skin side up on a small cooking sheet in the oven with the sweet potatoes. Roast about 10-12 minutes, or until skin begins to blister. Remove and place in a sealable plastic bag. Allow to sweat about 5 minutes. Remove and peel skin. Cut into strips. Next, place the red bell pepper and roasted chili in a small mixing bowl. Add the vinegar, a little salt and pepper, and set aside.

3. To toast pecans, heat sauté pan on medium heat. Add pecans and toast, stirring frequently to prevent burning, until fragrant, about 5 minutes. Remove and set aside. Remove potatoes from the oven when they are tender and stir in the roasted pepper mixture, check for seasoning, and transfer to a serving platter. Sprinkle with the pecans and parsley.

Walk through the front doors of the mid-century modern Hotel Valley Ho and you might be stunned by the 1950s beauty, grab a table at the hotel's restaurant, Café ZuZu, for approachable American fare that feels as classic as the surroundings. Chef Chuck Wiley, known for his ability to blend local, seasonal ingredients into time-honored favorites flirt with nostalgia on stand-out dishes such as his Roasted Tomato and Goat Cheese Casserole. Save room; you'll want to wash it all down with ZuZu's classic root beer float.

ROASTED LEG OF CHURRO LAMB
WITH HEIRLOOM BORDAL BEANS

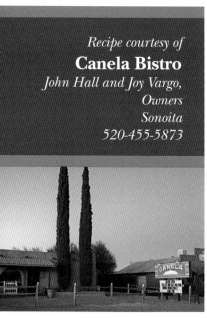

Recipe courtesy of
Canela Bistro
John Hall and Joy Vargo,
Owners
Sonoita
520-455-5873

Uncover the charm of the Southwest just one hour south of Tucson at Canela Bistro. This quaint sun- bleached brick adobe is filled with Native American trinkets like plants, pottery, artwork and bold colors—all as part of the effort to remain as locally focused as possible. Canela Bistro proudly features locally produced foods and wines, changing seasonally, and showcasing dishes such as fresh house-made pappardelle pasta, adobo-braised lamb shank and pan-seared mahi-mahi.

SERVES 6

2 tablespoons	olive oil
1 pound	wild amaranth leaves or spinach
6 tablespoons	roasted garlic
1/2 cup	prunes, soaked in hot water
2 ounces	chihuacle Negro chile
2 ounces	chile Negro (pasilla) chile
1 tablespoon	Kosher salt
1	leg Churro lamb, about 5-6 pounds, bones removed and butterflied (or substitute any leg of lamb)
	Kosher salt and pepper to taste
	Butcher twine

BEANS

1 pound	Bordal beans, soaked overnight
1 tablespoon	olive oil
1	large white onion, diced
3	fresh chile de arbol
10 cups	vegetable or chicken stock or water
1 bottle (12 ounces)	Tecate beer
1 pound	winter greens, such as lacinato kale, Swiss chard, dandelion greens or spinach
	Kosher salt

Note: Ask a butcher to remove the femur and aitch bone of the leg, or purchase the leg already de-boned.

1. Preheat oven to 350 degrees. Heat large sauté pan on medium-high heat. Add oil, and when hot, sauté roasted garlic with amaranth or spinach until tender, about 5-7 minutes. Set aside.

2. In a blender, puree soaked prunes and dried chiles until the consistency of paste and season with 1 tablespoon of kosher salt. Season the leg with a teaspoon salt and pepper, place cool spinach and garlic mixture into the cavity and tie with butcher twine.

3. Sear outside of leg in a cast iron pan until nicely browned and crispy. Then smear prune and chile mixture onto leg and place in an oven. Roast about 90 minutes, or until the internal temperature reaches 130 degrees. Remove and allow to rest before slicing. A beautiful sweet and spicy crust should form on the leg's surface.

Note: Bordal beans are a large white runner bean sometimes called "Mortage Lifters" due to their large size. Navy beans, cannellini beans or other white beans can be substituted.

4. Soak the beans overnight. In a large stockpot, add oil and, when hot, add onions and chile de arbol. Sauté about 5 minutes, or until onions are soft and translucent. Add the beans, then stock or water, bring to a simmer, and cook for 1 to 2 hours or until beans are tender. Add beer, continue to simmer, and add salt to taste only when the beans are completely cooked. Finally, before serving, add the roughly chopped greens to beans. Simmer for about 10 minutes before serving.

ESTELLA'S RED CHILE BEEF TAMALES

Recipe courtesy of
**Carolina's
Mexican Food**
*Angela Hernandez-Brown,
Owner
Phoenix
602-252-1503*

"*My name is Angela Hernandez-Brown and I am the current co-owner of The Original Carolina's Mexican Food at 1202 East Mohave Street in Phoenix along with my two sisters, Jennifer and Josephine.*

Carolina Valenzuela is our grandmother who in the early 1970s, along with her mother—our great-grandmother, Elvira Castellanos—showed our mother Estella LeGrande the tamale paste recipe and the techniques used in making these special tamale treats. My great-grand-mother, Anita Encinas, also taught Estella how to perfect her masa mix also. These three women cultivated a love of tamales in our mother.

Measuring ingredients and mixing to taste, then finding her way to make them just right for her family, our mother has perfected her tamales. This is my mother's red chile beef tamale recipe and all who taste these treasures at Christmas time will never forget how wonderful they truly are."

MAKES 4 DOZEN

BONELESS ROAST

5 pounds	boneless chuck roast (or your favorite beef roast)
3	cloves garlic
2 tablespoons	garlic powder
1/4	medium yellow onion
1/2 tablespoon	black pepper
2 tablespoons	salt

1. To cook roast, place it in pot and fill water to cover, almost to top of pot. Add both forms of garlic, onion, pepper and salt. Bring to boil on high then reduce to medium-low boil for up to 1 1/2 hours.

2. Cool roast and set 1/4 of the broth aside for later use in dough, and 3/4 for making red chile. When roast is cooled, cube beef into 1-inch pieces and set aside until mixed with red chile.

RED CHILE POD PASTE

8 to 10	dried chile pods
2	garlic cloves
2 teaspoons	salt
3 cups	boiled chile pod broth

3. To make the paste, place stemmed chile pods into pot and fill with water to cover pods. Bring to a boil, then reduce to low boil until tender. Save half the broth from chile pods.

4. Place half of the tender chile pods into blender, adding 1 1/2 cup chile broth, 1 garlic clove and 1 teaspoon salt. Purée ingredients in blender up to a minute. Pour chile paste into a separate container. Repeat this process with remaining half of chile pods and ingredients.

RED CHILE BEEF

	All saved purée chile pod paste
1/3 cup	cooking oil
1/3 cup	flour
2 teaspoons	garlic powder
1 teaspoon	salt
3/4	saved roast beef broth
	All cubed roast beef

5. To make the red chile beef, pour oil into 5-quart cooking pot on low heat; add flour and mix well into a smooth paste. Mix in all chile pod paste using whip; pour in beef broth until pot is 3/4 full. Turn heat up to medium-high and continue to stir until chile reaches a thick gravy consistency.

6. Add all cubed roast beef, stir gently with spoon. Set aside for tamale filling later.

CORN MASA

5 pounds	unprepared fresh white corn tamale dough (Corn Masa)
1 pound	lard (room temperature)
1 tablespoon	baking powder
2 teaspoons	salt
1 to 2 cups	roast beef broth

7. To make corn masa, break up masa into large bowl to a crumbly texture. Sprinkle in baking powder and add salt. Mix in thoroughly with hands. It is important that baking powder be mixed in well.

8. Add room temperature lard to bowl and mix very thoroughly with hands, leaving no lard pieces to be seen or felt in corn masa.

9. Now get your saved roast beef broth and add corn masa in 1/4-cup increments. A little broth will go a long way here. Using hands, work broth into masa thoroughly. It's ok to switch to a large mixing spoon as corn masa gets easier to work with. The texture should be smooth paste and not runny or loose.

CORN HUSKS AND PARCHMENT

1 pound	packaged corn husks
	9x9 parchment paper wraps

10. Clean and soak husks in warm water about 30-60 minutes until soft.

11. Shake off excess water, then spread corn masa onto corn husks. Portion out husks from warm water as needed. Corn husks should be same size as your hand's width; this makes for easy control when spreading corn masa. You will also spread smaller-width husks when needed to help in closing tamales. Using a workable large soup spoon or a small serving spoon, spread an even layer of corn masa across husk in right to left sweeps leaving 3-4 inches on top and 1-1/2 inch on bottom for folding tamale in parchment wrap. Set masa spread husks on work area

12. Fill center husks with moderate spoonful of red chile beef mixture, fold husk over to close; be careful not smash down tamale; if needed, use smaller husks for closure here. Repeat process of filling moderate spoonful of red chile beef until all masa spread husks are used.

13. Dampen all of wraps at one time with water, leaving 3x3 corner areas dry. Be careful not to over-wet for the water will travel upwards into the dry corner area. You will need a dry corner to grab and separate for wrapping tamales.

14. On your work area, lay filled tamale over middle part of parchment, fold wrap over tamale, then wrap bottom 1 inch of tamale folding over with wrap; do the same for top portion of tamale also, holding firmly so tamale will not unroll.

15. You may place tamales in freezer as you wrap or after a dozen are wrapped. Wrapped red beef tamales may be steamed as they are made, or frozen and steamed at later time.

This South Phoenix institution is famous for its ethereal flour tortillas, used to wrap the restaurant's mighty burritos and sold by the dozen for take-home. Back in the '50s, Carolina and Manuel Valenzuela began selling tortillas, tamales and burritos from their car, opening their first tiny restaurant in 1968 and moving to larger digs in 1972. When Manuel passed away in 1979, Carolina's children and grandchildren (particularly her son Joe) helped her run the business, and when the City of Phoenix purchased the property to expand the airport in 1985, Carolina's moved to its current home. Carolina passed away in 2002, but her descendents have stayed true to her philosophy, opening a second location in North Phoenix in 2005.

CAJUN SHRIMP DIANE

Recipe courtesy of
**Charlie Clark's
Steak House**
*Bill and Tricia Gibson,
Owners
Pinetop*
928-367-4900

As the oldest continuously operating restaurant in the White Mountains, this 74-year-old steakhouse is a beloved institution, built around the two original log cabins once used by bootlegger Jack Renfro, who poured moonshine from a barrel hidden beneath the bar. Charlie Clark bought the property in 1938 and turned it into a warm, rustic steakhouse, and although the rambling old place had a succession of owners after his death in 1952, it's been in the capable hands of Bill and Tricia Gibson for 30 years. Cajun Shrimp Diane is a spicy Charlie Clark's classic, great with pasta, rice or French bread.

SERVES 4

24	jumbo shrimp, uncooked, peeled and deveined
3/4 cup	butter or margarine, about 1 1/2 sticks, melted
	Cajun spice
4 cloves	fresh garlic, diced
4 bulbs	fresh shallots, diced
16	large fresh mushrooms, sliced

1. Dip shrimp in melted butter or margarine. Set aside butter for use later. Then dip in Cajun spice to coat. Set aside. In a separate pot, boil water. Once water reaches a boil, add a tablespoon of salt, then add linguine and cook 7–8 minutes or until al dente. Strain, setting 1/2 cup of pasta water aside. Place linguine aside. If necessary, periodically pour some water over pasta to keep from sticking.

2. Pour remaining melted butter into large skillet over medium heat. Add shrimp, garlic, shallots, and mushrooms. Simmer until shrimp are cooked and turn pink, about 3-4 minutes. Additional melted butter may be added to pan if more "sauce" is desired.

3. Pour sauce and shrimp over linguine and toss. Divide pasta and shrimp mixture into 4 equal portions and serve.

TRUFFLE-INFUSED PRIME SIRLOIN
SERVED WITH FAREKI, SHALLOT CONFIT, AND A RED WINE SAUCE

Recipe courtesy of
**Christopher's &
Crush Lounge**
*Chef Christopher Gross
Phoenix
602-522-2344*

SERVES 4

4 pieces, about 4 ounces each	sirloin lightly smoked in cold smoke for 5 minutes *(Heat wood chips in wok and remove from heat. Place sirloin on a grill over wok to smoke.)*
2-3 tablespoons	truffle oil
	Salt and pepper to taste
3 tablespoons	peeled and chopped shallots
1 sprig	fresh thyme
4 grinds	black pepper
3 cups	red wine, such as Merlot
3 cups	veal or chicken stock
2 or more tablespoons	unsalted butter
	Salt and pepper to taste
1 tablespoon	olive oil
1/3 cup	peeled and finely minced freshly cut shallots
	Salt and pepper to taste
2 tablespoons	chopped fresh chives
3/4 pound (about 2 cups)	fareki
1 tablespoon	olive oil
2 tablespoons	peeled and minced garlic
5 tablespoons	peeled and minced shallots
3 cups	warm chicken stock
	Salt and pepper to taste
3 tablespoons	chopped fresh chives

1. Cover beef with truffle oil. Cover and refrigerate for at least 1 day. Season meat with salt and pepper. Heat a large skillet to medium high heat. Add olive oil, and when hot add sirloin. Brown all sides. Remove and carefully spoon out any browning fat, leaving behind the meat juices. Set pas aside.

2. Heat the same skillet to medium high heat to make red wine sauce. When hot, add shallots. Stir for several minutes to soften, but do not brown. Add thyme, pepper and red wine. Bring to a boil, reduce heat to medium low and cook until reduced in half. Add stock and boil slowly until reduced to 1/2 cup. Transfer to a saucepan and set aside.

3. To cook sirloin, heat oven to 375 degrees. Place browned loin in a large roasting pan in the middle level of a preheated 375 degree oven and roast to rare or medium rare—about 120-130 degrees on an instant meat thermometer. When done, remove the meat to a cutting board and allow to rest while deglazing the roasting pan.

4. To deglaze, place pan on stovetop burner on medium high heat. Add 1 cup of red wine and scrape up any roasting juices and meat tidbits. Transfer this winy pan juice to the wine and shallot sauce; boil rapidly to reduce to 1 cup or so.

5. For shallot confit, heat sauté pan on medium. Add oil, and when hot add shallots. Sauté until tender and translucent, about 6-8 minutes. Season lightly with salt and pepper. Set aside. Reheat just before serving, and blend in the minced chives.

6. Place fareki in a large sieve. Place sieve over a bowl of cold water, swish water around grain and drain well. Heat a heavy-bottomed 8-inch pan about 2 inches deep over medium heat. Add the oil, stir in the fareki, and sauté for several minutes. The grain should be toasted, but not burned. Stir in the garlic, shallots and warm stock. Bring to boil and reduce to slow simmer and cover. Simmer covered for 35-45 minutes, adding a little more stock if fareki becomes too dry. Season with salt and pepper to taste and stir in chives before serving.

7. To serve, reheat the sautéed shallot confit. Cut the beef into thin slices and arrange on plate, ringing the meat with the red wine sauce and garnishing with chopped shallots.

Whether they want to relax in the chic, contemporary dining room, find a perch at the sleek kitchen bar overlooking the exhibition kitchen, join friends in the private dining room, or cozy up with a glass of wine in Crush Lounge, guests inevitably linger at Chef Christopher Gross's eponymous eatery for his masterful French cuisine. While his career has taken him to Los Angeles, London and Paris, Gross returned to Phoenix in 1983, going on to win a James Beard Award and countless accolades from the likes of Food + Wine, Esquire, *and* Gourmet. *His decadent sirloin dish is one of his favorite recipes, and also the one he cooked with legendary chef Julia Child at her home and for her renowned PBS series.*

PAN-SEARED SCALLOPS
WITH ROASTED CORN GRITS, SNOW PEA GREENS AND RED ROCK COLA GASTRIQUE

Recipe courtesy of
Citizen Public House
Chef Bernie Kantak
Scottsdale
480-398-4208

Informally known by many as a pub, a "public house" is the proper name for a drinking establishment in Britain. Chef Bernie Kantak was part of the culinary team who created the landmark restaurant Cowboy Ciao in the late '90s and has reinvented not only himself, but the traditional public house by giving it a new-fangled, modern edge with Citizen Public House. Monochrome white walls give the restaurant a very streamlined feel, highlighted by burly chapel beams draping over a stainless steel-topped bar. The restaurant offers familiar favorites like the Original Chopped Salad, as well as unique twists on classic pub fare such as Pork Belly Pastrami, Fair Trade Coffee Charred Short Ribs and a lamb burger.

SERVES 4

12	scallops
	Salt and pepper
	Olive oil as needed

GRITS

1/4 cup	roasted corn
1/2 cup	heavy cream
1/2 cup	chicken stock
1/8 cup	grits
	Salt and pepper to taste
1 tablespoon	butter

SAUTÉ SNOW PEA GREENS

1 cup	snow pea greens
	Oil as needed
	Salt and pepper to taste

COLA GASTRIQUE

1/2 cup	cola
1/2 cup	balsamic
2 tablespoons	ketchup

1. Season each scallop with salt and pepper, and place in a sauté pan on high heat with enough oil to lightly coat the bottom of the pan. Cook roughly 1 1/2 minutes on each side, or until the scallop is seared. Remove and keep warm.

2. Lightly coat corn cob with vegetable oil. Heat outdoor grill to medium high heat. Add corn cob and roast about 10 minutes, turning frequently, until nearly half the kernels are scorched. Remove from grill and cut kernels off the cob.

3. To make grits, combine cream and stock in small saucepan and bring to boil. Whisk in grits and corn. Return to simmer and cook until mixture has thickened, stirring frequently to avoid burning or sticking. Season and finish with butter.

4. In hot sauté pan add a touch of oil and snow pea greens. Season with salt and pepper, stir and sauté for about 60 seconds. Keep warm until serving.

5. In small saucepan, combine cola, balsamic and ketchup, bring to boil, reduce to simmer and reduce to syrupy consistency.

6. To serve, place grits on 4 plates. Top with scallops and snow peas. Drizzle Cola Gastrique over dish and serve.

GORGONZOLA-ENCRUSTED TENDERLOIN FILET

Recipe courtesy of
The Cottage Place
Chef Frank Branham
Flagstaff
928-774-8431

Ensconced in a cozy bungalow built in 1909, Flagstaff's oldest fine dining venue deftly combines French classics with a modern American sensibility. Chef-owner Frank Branham, who tends his own garden, sources local ingredients and makes mozzarella in-house, created this dish for a food-and-wine-pairing class to demonstrate that blue cheese softens the tannins in red wine. "As I served samples, a chorus of 'wows' moved across the room," he says, "and I knew immediately this dish had to be on the menu." It's now a Cottage Place signature, best served with a big Cabernet.

SERVES 4

1/4 cup	panko breadcrumbs
4	tenderloin filets, about 6 ounces each
	Salt to taste
	Fresh ground black pepper to taste
	Vegetable oil spray as needed
1 cup	Gorgonzola Mousse (see recipe)
1 cup	Port Beurre Rouge (see recipe)

GORGONZOLA MOUSSE

1/2 cup	gorgonzola cheese, crumbled
1/2 cup	cream cheese, softened
1/8 teaspoon	black pepper
1/2 teaspoon	Worcestershire Sauce

PORT BEURRE ROUGE

1 cup	port wine
2	small shallots, about 2 tablespoons, minced
2 tablespoons	heavy cream
1/2 pound	unsalted butter, chilled and cut in cubes
	Kosher salt, as needed
	Pepper to taste

1. Preheat grill to high and oven to 400 degrees. Heat a large sauté pan over medium heat. Add bread crumbs and stir constantly until golden brown. Set aside.

2. Season each filet with salt and pepper. Spray each filet with vegetable oil. Place filets on hot grill for 2 to 3 minutes, then turn each filet 90 degrees to create diamond-shaped char marks. Continue grilling for 2 to 3 minutes. Flip filets over to other side and repeat the process.

3. Remove filets one stage more rare than desired doneness and place in oven proof baking dish. Let filets rest for 2 to 3 minutes.

4. To make the mousse, in separate bowl mix gorgonzola, cream cheese, black pepper and Worcestershire and stir thoroughly.

5. To make the Port Beurre Rouge, combine port and shallots in a small saucepan. Bring to a boil, reduce heat, and simmer until reduced in volume by half. Add heavy cream and simmer until reduced in volume by half. Remove from the heat. Add several cubes of butter and whisk until incorporated, keeping sauce between 105 and 125 degrees to prevent sauce from breaking. Return the pan to the heat if it gets too cool to melt the butter. Continue whisking in the remaining butter until it has all been absorbed. Strain sauce and season with salt and pepper. Serve immediately or store for up to two hours in an insulated container.

6. After, top each filet with a quarter of the Gorgonzola Mousse and a quarter of the toasted bread crumbs.

7. Bake filets in a 400-degree oven until mousse is hot and soft. Be careful to not overcook as mousse will become runny and slide off.

8. Serve each filet in a pool of Port Beurre Rouge.

NOTES:
Port Beurre Rouge –
This butter sauce adds a subtle richness to meat or seafood dishes, allowing their natural flavor to shine. Despite the fact that a butter sauce is essentially liquid butter, if you are careful to use a small amount it will add richness, without going overboard with the calories.

Butter Sauces are very fragile and can easily break, turning them into clear butter and a foamy residue. However, there are two tricks that will help you avoid that crisis. First, once you start adding butter, keep the sauce between 105 and 125 degrees by moving it on and off the heat. Second, as soon as you have added the last of the butter, pour the sauce into a pre-heated, insulated container. If you can serve it from that container it would be even safer.

PUERCO LENTO

Recipe courtesy of
Cowboy Ciao
Chef Lester Gonzalez
Scottsdale
480-946-3111

SERVES 4

1	pork shank
1 teaspoon	toasted cumin
1/2 teaspoon	smoked paprika
1/2 teaspoon	garlic granules
1/2 teaspoon	onion granules
1/2 teaspoon	oregano
1 tablespoon	salt
1/2 teaspoon	black pepper

FINGERLING POTATOES

13	fingerling potatoes, sliced 1/4-inch thick
1/2	small yellow onion, medium diced
1 tablespoon	minced garlic
3 tablespoons	oil

WINE SAUCE

3	shallots, roasted in oven, then sliced
1/4 cup	red wine
1/4 cup	red wine vinegar
1/2 cup	molasses

CREAM SAUCE

1 cup	heavy cream
3	Hatch chilies, roasted and peeled, and diced small
3/4 cup	white cheddar
	Salt and pepper to taste

1. Preheat oven to 300 degrees. Mix spices together in a small bowl and rub on shank. Then tightly wrap in plastic wrap, wrap in aluminum foil and place in oven and slow cook for 5 hours. In medium bowl toss together potatoes, onions, garlic and oil. Roast at 300 degrees for about 30-40 minutes, or until potatoes easily pierce with a fork. When done, remove from oven, set aside.

2. Place shallots, red wine and vinegar and molasses in a saucepot. Simmer and reduce to syrup, stirring occasionally. Remove and chill. In a sauté pan bring cream to a boil. Add cheese, chilies, then potatoes, add salt and pepper to taste.

What began in 1997 as a cheeky hotspot with a trio of influences (Mexico, Italy, and the American Southwest) has evolved into an Old Town Scottsdale destination serving globally inspired modern American cuisine. Along with its eclectic dishes, Cowboy Ciao's serious staying power has had much to do with long-time (former) partner Marianne Belardi's warmth and owner Peter Kasperski's dedication to fine wines; the restaurant won a Wine Spectator award in its first year of operation, and has been raking in the accolades ever since. Accordingly, chef Lester Gonzalez creates bold, explosive flavor profiles that pair beautifully with the wines, as exemplified by this slow-cooked pork with a chile kick.

RASPBERRY PLUM BBQ RIBS

SERVES 10-12

6	rack ribs, use a fresh rib if possible with an average weight of 1.75 pounds a rack. These cuts of ribs usually have more meat and less bone.

DRY RUB

3 cups	Spike Seasoning (Available at Bashas or Whole Foods Market)
2 pounds	turbanado or raw sugar
1 cup	Kosher salt
1/2 cup	smoked paprika
1/2 cup	dry oregano
1/2 cup	New Mexican chili powder

BBQ SAUCE

1 quart	red onions roasted until translucent, about 40 minutes in a 375 degree oven, and quarted
1 quart	red plums, canned or fresh
2 cups	fire roasted tomatoes, canned or fresh
1/2 cup	raspberry vinegar
1/4 cup	pureed chipotle peppers (preferably Embassa)
2 cups	dark beer
2 quarts	ketchup
2 cups	fresh orange juice
1/4 cup	Franks Red Hot Sauce
1/2 cup	Grandmas Molasses
1 cup	raspberry puree
1/4 cup	Worcestershire
1/4 cup	yellow mustard
8	cloves roasted garlic, pre-roasted
1/4 cup	chili powder
2 pounds	brown sugar

Recipe courtesy of
Cowboy Club
Chef Chris Dobrowolski
Sedona
928-282-4200

Cowboy grub doesn't get much classier than at the Cowboy Club in Uptown Sedona. Almost every dish is infused with a touch of Southwestern flare and flavor like prickly pear, chipotle, green and poblano chiles, rattlesnake, buffalo and nopales cactus. The Cowboy Clubs boasts more than just decadent dishes, such as their Raspberry Plum BBQ Ribs, which are also featured at their sister restaurant: Barking Frog Grille; Cowboy Club is also home to the second largest set of Texas Longhorns in the United States.

1. For the rub, mix all ingredients thoroughly.

2. To prepare the BBQ sauce, add all ingredients to a large saucepan on medium low. Bring to a simmer and cook for 30-45 minutes or until ingredients are tender. Next, puree with in a blender, food processor or hand-held mixer. Return to pot after ingredients are pureed and simmer again until the sauce sticks to the back of a wooden spoon. Remove from heat and cool as quickly possible to less than 40 degrees. This recipe makes approximately 1 1/2 gallons when complete. Cover and refrigerate leftover sauce for future use.

3. Preheat oven to 250 degrees. To prepare the ribs, thoroughly coat both sides of your ribs with the dry rub from above. Place in a roasting pan with 2 cups of water in the bottom. Cover ribs with parchment paper first, then plastic wrap, and then aluminum foil. Bake at 250 degrees for 8 hours or until fork tender. When ribs are done in the oven finish on a medium high grill, basting with the BBQ sauce until sauce is caramelized.

TUSCAN TOMATO PESTO ZUPPA

Recipe courtesy of
Dahl and DiLuca
Chef Lisa Dahl
Sedona
928-284-3010

When Lisa Dahl and Andrea Di Luca opened charming Dahl & Di Luca in 1996, they created an upscale Italian restaurant specializing in lusty, straight-forward dishes and classy but comfortable vibe. Locals arrived in droves, as did out-of-town visitors, making this multi-award-winning restaurant one of the most popular in Sedona. In 2003, Dahl and her partner opened Cucina Rustica, a stunning ode to Italy that manages to be rustic and elegant at once. This recipe may be found on the menus at both restaurants—reconfigured by season and whim.

SERVES 4

2	large carrots (about 8 ounces)
2	large fresh shallots
4 to 5	cloves garlic
1/2 cup	extra virgin olive oil
1/4 teaspoon	crushed red pepper
1 ounce	chopped, packed fresh basil
2 cans (29-ounces)	San Marzano imported tomatoes in juice with basil
2 tablespoons	pesto
8 cups	chicken or vegetable broth
1/4 teaspoon	black pepper
1/2 to 1 cup	cream (optional)

1. Peel the carrots and cut them into chunks. Place them in a food processor and mince to a medium pulp. Scoop out and set aside in a bowl.

2. Finely mince the shallots and garlic by hand or in the same processor used for carrots. Set aside for sautéing.

3. In a stockpot (preferably enamel or stainless steel, not aluminum) place 1/4 cup of the olive oil and heat until smoking. Add chopped carrots and reduce heat to medium high. Constantly stir to keep from browning too quickly or burning. When carrots turn golden in color, add the minced shallots and garlic. Add a little more olive oil and continue cooking until mirepoix is evenly coated, soft and colored, about 5-7 minutes. This caramelization sets the flavor, and overcooking taints the soup flavor.

4. When done, add the crushed red pepper and fresh basil, stirring quickly to not burn. Next, add the tomatoes and raise the heat to sear them but not to burn the fresh basil, then bring to a boil. Continually stir the bottom of pan to keep the sediment from burning. Then lower to a simmer and cook for 1 hour, or as long as needed to bring out the robust color.

STUFFED FRENCH TOAST

Recipe courtesy of
Darbi's Café
Darbi Komzelman, Owner
Pinetop
928-367-6556

Huge pancakes, eggs sunny-side up, crispy hash browns, and biscuits and homemade sausage gravy are just a taste of some of the scrumptious breakfast classics served at Darbi's Café. You'll want to arrive early, because this breakfast spot is an all-time favorite of locals as well as those passing through. The quaint space is decorated with vintage birdcages reminiscent of your great-aunt's house. You can spot owner Darbi on a daily basis, running around, clearing tables, working the register, and, of course, greeting guests.

SERVES 4

2 cups	fresh blueberries, plus extra for garnish
1 cup	water
3/4 cup	sugar
1/4 cup	water
3 tablespoon	cornstarch
4	eggs
2/3 cup	milk
2 teaspoon	cinnamon
1 teaspoon	nutmeg
1 1/2 teaspoon	vanilla
2 tablespoons	butter
8	thick slices of bread
	Fresh whipped cream
	Blueberries for garnish

1. To prepare filling, in saucepan over medium heat combine blueberries, 1 cup water and sugar. Bring to a boil. In a separate bowl, combine 1/4 cup water and cornstarch. Slowly add to saucepan to thicken.

2. Heat griddle to medium heat. Mix eggs, milk, cinnamon, nutmeg and vanilla in bowl. Melt butter on griddle. Dip bread into egg mix and place on buttered griddle. Let cook 3-5 minutes and flip and cook an additional 3-5 minutes.

3. Take 2 slices cooked French toast and make a pocket in the center of one. Fill with blueberry filling and whipped cream. Top this with your other slice of French toast. Finish off with whipped cream and fresh blueberries.

GREEN GAZPACHO

Recipe courtesy of
Diablo Burger
Chef Todd Griffith
Flagstaff
928-724-3274

SERVES 4-6

3 pounds	plum tomatoes
4	tomatillos
2	cucumbers
1	red bell pepper
1	green bell pepper
1	serrano chile (optional)
1	sweet onion
1	clove of garlic
1 cup	white wine (Page Spring Cellars Vino del Barrio Blanca is an excellent choice-drink the rest!)
2 tablespoons	white wine vinegar
1 tablespoon	sherry vinegar
1 tablespoon	honey
	Juice of 1 lemon
2	avocados
1 bunch	cilantro
1 bunch	scallions
	Sea salt

1. Core the tomatoes and cut into quarters. Place the quartered tomatoes in a food processor and process to a pulp. Set a colander lined with butter muslin or fine cheesecloth over a large bowl. Place the tomato pulp into the colander and allow the clear juice to drain from the tomatoes into the bowl. The tomato juice may need to be filtered more than once to achieve clarity. The tomatoes must produce 2 cups of liquid.

2. Peel, core and finely dice the tomatillos. Peel, de-seed and dice the cucumbers. Remove the stems, seeds and dice the red and green bell peppers and optional serrano chile. Finely dice the sweet onion. Mince the clove of garlic.

3. Combine all of the vegetables from step 2 in a large bowl. Add the white wine, white wine vinegar, sherry vinegar, honey and lemon juice. Stir and set aside.

4. Chop 1 avocado into large chunks and place into a clean food processor along with the 2 cups of clear tomato juice. Scrape down the sides as needed, until the juice is smooth.

5. With the tomato juice/avocado mixture still in the food processor, add one-third of the chopped vegetable mixture and process until fine. Add another third of the vegetable mixture to the food processor and pulse a few times.

6. Lastly, add the contents of the food processor to the bowl with the remaining third of the vegetable mixture, and add sea salt to taste. Place the gazpacho in the refrigerator for 4-6 hours before serving to allow the flavors to meld. Adjust the seasoning before service.

7. When ready to serve, dice the other avocado, and chop the cilantro and scallions. Place each into separate serving dishes. Serve the Gazpacho in chilled bowls, and allow your guests to garnish with the avocado, cilantro and scallions.

Owner Derrick Widmark makes sustainability his mantra at this casual but decidedly upscale burger joint, where the grass-fed, hormone- and antibiotic-free beef he uses is sourced from two historic Northern Arizona ranches—Flying M and Bar T Bar, both founding members of a grassroots collaborative devoted to stewardship of the land. Although burgers are Diablo's raison d'être, this keep-it-real and keep-it-local operation is also famous for seasonal soups, including this summer favorite, which uses ingredients sourced from McClendon's Select, Page Springs Cellars and the Flagstaff Farmer's Market.

DURANT'S ORIGINAL CHEESECAKE

Recipe courtesy of
Durant's
Carol McElroy, proprietor
Phoenix
602-264-5967

SERVES 8-10

CRUST

6 tablespoons	butter
1 1/2 cups	finely crushed graham cracker crumbs
1/3 cup	sugar

FILLING

2 packages (8 ounces)	Philadelphia Cream Cheese, softened
1 cup	sugar
1 pint	sour cream
1 teaspoon	vanilla

Enter through the backdoor of this 60-year-old steakhouse and you'll feel like Henry Hill, infamous "Goodfellas" mobster who had unparalleled access to stylish kitchen entrances. As in the movie, the unassuming exterior gives way to a red carpet leading into the kitchen where, after dodging a few chefs, you'll find yourself transported to the 1950s by an interior of velvet wallpaper, dim lighting and an honest, well-worn staff. Dive into the complimentary garlic-and-herb-soaked bread before summoning a plate of oysters Rockefeller, a porterhouse steak and a glass of bourbon.

1. Melt 6 tablespoons of butter in a saucepan. In a bowl, mix finely crushed graham cracker crumbs and sugar. Pour in melted butter, and mix until graham crackers are completely coated and moist. Press into sides of an eight inch spring form pan.

2. Preheat oven to 275 degrees. In mixing bowl with mixer set at low speed, cream Philadelphia cream cheese until very smooth with no lumps. Add 1 cup of sugar, blend completely. Remove 3-4 tablespoons of sour cream from pint and set aside in small bowl. Add pint of sour cream, blend at slow speed until well blended. Add teaspoon of vanilla blend well. Pour filling into prepared spring form pan.

3. Bake 1 hour. Filling will "shimmy" and appear soft in center. Gently spread 3-4 tablespoons of room temperature sour cream over the top of the cake. Allow to cool on counter for an hour. Refrigerate overnight or until thoroughly chilled.

BACON-INFUSED MEATLOAF

Recipe courtesy of
Eddie's House
Chef Eddie Matney
Scottsdale
480-946-1622

SERVES 4

1 pound	bacon, cut into 1-inch pieces
1	medium red onion, chopped
2 1/2 pounds	ground chuck beef
4 ounces	ounces fresh basil, chopped
3	Roma tomatoes, chopped
3	eggs
1 1/2 cups	cups panko bread crumbs
1/2 teaspoon	salt
1/4 teaspoon	pepper

1. Preheat oven to 350 degrees. Place onions, and bacon in a sauté pan, cook until onions become translucent, about 5-7 minutes. In a separate bowl, mix onion-bacon mixture with remaining ingredients. Mix well.

2. Put into bread loaf pan, bake at 350 degrees for 40 minutes

Eddie Matney is a chef with a dynamic persona and equally eccentric cuisine. His restaurant, Eddie's House, is a studio of remarkable creativity. His culinary bravado transcends cultures; fusing sweet with savory, East with West, Southwestern with island influence, Mediterranean with American staples, comfort food with modern touches and traditional fare with guilty pleasures. Matney's unconventional flavors and welcoming surroundings have kept Valley diners coming back time and time again for years.

ENCHILADA SONORENSES AND SALSA DE CHILE COLORADO

FLAT CORN MASA PATTIES WITH RED CHILE SAUCE

Recipe courtesy of
El Charro Café
Carlotta Flores
Tucson
520-622-1922

The Flores Family has been at the helm of the oldest, continuously family-owned and operated Mexican restaurant in the United States, and for several generations has been turning the wheel of Tucson's hospitality community. El Charro Café, a unique Tucson-brand of eatery, is overseen by Chef Carlotta Flores. Carlotta's admiration for food, culture, history and Tucson, infuses every dish she creates, every customer she greets, and every connection she makes within the community.

SERVES 6-8

ENCHILADA SONORENSES

1	medium potato cooked
2 pounds	fresh corn masa
1 teaspoon	salt
1/2 teaspoon	baking soda
1/2 cup	shredded cheese
	Oil for frying

GARNISH:

4 cups	salsa de chili Colorado
1 cup	sliced green olives
1 cup	chopped green onions
1 cup	shredded longhorn or cojita cheese
1 ounce	vinegar
1 tablespoon	dried oregano
1-2 heads	iceberg lettuce or green cabbage, shredded
	Sliced radish
	Lime slice

SALSA DE CHILE COLORADO (Makes about 2 quarts)

12	dried, red chiles
2 quarts	water, boiling
3 tablespoons	oil
1/4 cup	garlic puree
1/2 teaspoon	salt, or to taste
3 tablespoons	flour

1. Peel potato and cut into quarters. Bring a small pot of salted water to a boil, add potatoes and cook about 10 minutes, or until potatoes can be pierced with a fork. Remove and grate potatoes in a potato ricer for food mill. Set aside. Mix masa, salt, soda, potato and cheese. Shape into balls the size of an egg. Place, one at a time, between two sheets of wax paper and flatten with a rolling pin or tortilla press to 4 or 5 inches in diameter, or 1/4-inch thick, whichever you arrive at first. Cover with damp paper towels.

2. Heat 1 inch of oil in small skillet and fry each patty 5 minutes on each side and drain on paper towels.

3. To make the salsa, rinse chiles in cold water and remove stems. Cook in boiling water until tender, about 15 minutes. Remove chiles and reserve cooking liquid. Place a few of the chiles in a blender or food processor with 1/2 cup reserve liquid, and blend to a paste. Remove to bowl. Repeat with remaining chiles. Heat oil in a large skillet. Add garlic puree and flour, stirring until flour browns. Add chile paste, stirring constantly until it boil and thickens. Season with salt. Thin slightly with cooking liquid.

4. Cover each patty with hot salsa de chile Colorado and top with olives, onion, and cheese. Mix vinegar and dried oregano in a small bowl and serve on the side with a bowl of shredded cheese. Garnish with lettuce, radish and lime slice.

EL CHORRO'S BEEF STROGANOFF

Recipe courtesy of
El Chorro
Chef Charles Kassels
Paradise Valley
480-948-5170

SERVES 4

4 tablespoons	olive oil
14 ounces	beef tenderloin, cut into 1/4 inch chunks
3/4 cup	diced white onions
3/4 cup	diced button mushrooms, washed, dried and diced
2	cloves garlic, diced
2 shallots	sliced thinly
1/2 cup	red sweet Vermouth
1 cup	sour cream, divided
1 1/4 cup	heavy cream
8 tablespoons	whole butter
3/4 cup	semi-glace
2 tablespoons	chopped parsley, thyme and dill
	Salt and pepper to taste
1/4 cup	diced sugar snap peas and baby carrots, slightly steamed to soften

1. In a large sauté pan on medium high heat, add olive oil, and when hot, sauté beef, onions and mushrooms until meat is dark brown and caramelized, about 8-10 minutes. Add garlic and shallots and continue to cook for 1 minute. Deglaze with Vermouth, stirring frequently, until pan is dry. Add butter, half the sour cream and all heavy cream and continue to cook until thick.

2. Add semi-glace, parsley, salt and pepper to taste.

3. Garnish with dollops of sour cream, peas and carrots, divide into 4 bowls.

Few Arizona restaurants boast the rich history of legendary El Chorro, which was originally built in 1934 as the Judson School for Girls and converted to a restaurant and lodge in 1937. Fewer still distinguish themselves with such a list of luminaries who've visited over the years, including Clark Gable, John Wayne and Milton Berle. Longtime El Chorro bartender Joe Miller and his wife, Evie (formerly a cocktail waitress there), purchased the property in the 1970s, expanding it into a year-round operation. And after Valley philanthropist Jacquie Dorrance acquired El Chorro in 2009, joined by partners Kristy and Tim Moore, the property was once again renovated by architect Mark Candelaria to include a number of green building features and 21st-century technologies. But the beef stroganoff is just as good as ever. Executive Chef Charles Kassels may have modernized the menu, but he kept the beloved classics.

FAJITAS

Recipe courtesy of
El Matador Restaurant
Mike Anagnopoulos, Owner
Phoenix
602-254-7563

A Downtown Phoenix landmark, El Matador has been feeding hungry guests its Americanized Mexican food since 1976 and continues to please with hot and crisp tortilla chips made in-house daily and an array of Mexican and American favorites. Red leather booths seat guests at spacious tables; a classic old-fashioned wooden bar serves one-heck-of-a strong margarita; and, as an alternative, there is a nice outdoor patio. As you walk into El Matador, glance to the right and check out the wall of autographed photos of the owner with local athletes, politicians and actors from over the years.

SERVES 4

8 ounces	sirloin steak
5 ounces	chicken breast
3/4	medium red onion, sliced
3/4	medium yellow onion, sliced
1	red bell pepper, sliced into strips
1	green bell pepper, sliced into strips
1 1/2 tablespoons	cilantro, chopped
	Salt, to taste
	Pepper, to taste
3 tablespoons	butter

1. Marinate steak and chicken breast in your favorite Italian dressing. On a grill, cook both steak and chicken till done to preference. Remove from grill and slice into strips.

2. Slice onions and peppers into strips. Add sliced onions, peppers, salt, pepper and cilantro to pan and sauté.

3. Take a sizzling hot iron skillet. Add butter, vegetables, and then, meat on top.

STUFFED GRAPE LEAVES

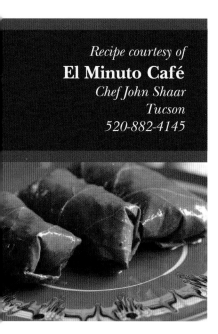

Recipe courtesy of
El Minuto Café
Chef John Shaar
Tucson
520-882-4145

Beirut-born John Shaar must've picked up an interest in Mexican food in El Paso, where he lived for a time before settling permanently in Tucson and opening El Minuto in 1936. It's been a Tucson standby ever since. In 1952, Shaar's son George took over the business with his wife Rosalva, who still runs the kitchen today with help from her daughter and granddaughter. Carne seca and chile rellenos are two of the house specialties.

SERVES 10

5 pounds	ground lamb
1/2 cup	pine nuts
1 cup	basmati rice
5 tablespoons	Lebanese 7 spice
1 bulb	garlic, peeled and chopped
1	white onion, chopped
	Juice of 1 lemon
	Salt and pepper to taste
5 jars (about 16 ounces)	grape leaves
2	lemons, cut in half
	Plain yogurt for serving

1. Place all ingredients except grape leaves, yogurt and lemon halves in a large mixing bowl. Mix until completely blended.

2. Place grape leaves on clean, flat surface. Fill with equal amounts of lamb and rice mixture. Roll grape leaves, and in batches, place in a tamale pot with 2 halved lemons, sprinkle with salt and pepper, and steam for about an hour, or until grape leaves are tender. Serve with yogurt.

SONORAN ENCHILADA

SERVES 4-6

1 pound	masa
1/2 teaspoon	baking powder
1/2 teaspoon	salt
1/2 cup	shredded cheddar cheese
	Canola oil for frying
	Canned enchilada sauce for dipping
	Diced onions, black olives and dill pickle for topping.

1. In a large mixing bowl, add masa, baking powder, salt and cheddar cheese. Mix well. Use hand to make a pancake-like patty, about 3 inches in diameter and 1/2 inch thick.

2. Heat sauté pan on medium high heat. Add a thin layer of oil, and when hot add masa pancakes, in batches, and fry until browned and crispy on both sides.

3. Dip the patty in enchilada sauce. Top with diced onions, diced black olives and diced dill pickle.

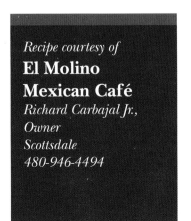

Recipe courtesy of
**El Molino
Mexican Café**
*Richard Carbajal Jr.,
Owner
Scottsdale
480-946-4494*

Housed in an old adobe, the original El Molino Mexican Café on South 22nd Street in Phoenix was opened by Joe and Rosa Carbajal in 1937 as a restaurant and market, selling staples such as masa, corn husks and spices to people who wanted to cook, as well as ready-made tamales and menudo to people who didn't. Joe, who had studied to be an engineer, also invented a refrigerated tamale-making machine to accommodate the crush of tamale orders at Christmas. In the late '80s, the Carbajals' grandson Richard opened a second location in Scottsdale, ten years before the original store closed for good. El Molino Mexican Café Scottsdale remains a popular go-to for tamales, chimis, chile rellenos and green chile.

PAN-SEARED SALMON TOSTADA

Recipe courtesy of
El Tovar
Chef Matt McTigue
Grand Canyon
928-638-2631

SERVES 4

1/2 cup	canola oil, divided
4	salmon filets, about 6-ounces each
6 ounces	spring or mesclun lettuce mix
1 Recipe	Chile Lime rice
1 Recipe	Lime Sour Cream, room temperature shake well before using
1 Recipe	Chile Olive Oil, from temperature shake well before using
1 Recipe	fire roasted corn salsa, room temperature and stir well before using
4	blue corn tortillas, 6-inches, baked crisp im a 350 degree oven for about 5-7 minutes
4	red corn tortillas 6-inches, and baked crisp in a 350 degree oven for about 5-7 minutes

CHILE OLIVE OIL

1 cup	olive oil
1 tablespoon	ancho chile paste
1 teaspoon	Tabasco

CHILE LIME RICE

1 tablespoon	cottonseed oil
1/2	yellow onion, small, diced
1/2 teaspoon	garlic, minced
2 tablespoons	tomato paste
	juice of 2 limes
3 cups	cooked white rice, room temperature
1/2 tablespoon	chili powder
1 teaspoon	chopped cilantro
	Salt and black pepper to taste

FIRE ROASTED CORN SALSA

	Canola oil for coating corn
3	ears fresh corn
1/2	jalapeño pepper, seeded, minced
1/4	green bell pepper, small dice
1/4	red bell pepper, small dice
1 tablespoon	cilantro, chopped
1/4	red onion, small dice
1/8 teaspoon	teaspoon salt, to taste
1/8 teaspoon	ground black pepper
1	tomato, diced medium
1/2 cup	vegetable juice

FOR LIME SOUR CREAM

1 cup	sour cream
2 tablespoons	lime juice

1. Heat sauté pan on medium high. Add enough canola oil to lightly cover pan, and when hot, add salmon. Sear, about 4 minutes a side, for medium rare. Remove from pan and keep warm while preparing the remainder of the dish.

2. To make Chile Olive Oil, combine all ingredients and mix well. Pour mixture into a plastic bottle with squirt top. Hold at room temperature. Shake well before using. Dress greens in chile olive oil in bowl, about 3 tablespoons of the oil. Set aside.

3. To make Chile Lime Rice, heat sauté pan over medium-high heat. Add oil and sauté onion until translucent, about 5 minutes. Add minced garlic and sauté until slightly browned, about 2 minutes. Add tomato paste and cook until it turns slightly brown and caramelizes, about 4-6 minutes. Deglaze tomato paste with fresh lime juice. Add cooked, room temperature rice and stir in until rice is hot. Add chili powder and chopped cilantro. Stir in. Season to your taste with salt and pepper. Hold warm for dinner service.

4. To make Fire Roasted Corn Salsa, heat grill of medium heat. Lightly coat corn cobs with oil and grill, turning frequently, until corn begins to char, about 5-7 minutes. Remove and allow to cool slightly. Use a sharp knife to remove corn from cob. Prepare all ingredients and reserve. Place corn and remaining ingredients in a bowl and mix thoroughly. Hold at room temperature for 1 hour.

5. To make Lime Sour Cream, mix ingredients in a bowl with a whisk until combined. Pour mixture into a plastic bottle with a squirt top. Place in refrigerator.

6. To assemble, place 1 of each tortilla at 4 and 8 o'clock on each plate. Divide greens evenly and top tortillas. Place medium rare salmon on top of greens. Top each piece of salmon with corn salsa. Place 3/8 cup portions of chile-lime rice on each plate at 12 o'clock. Squirt lime sour cream over salmon. Serve immediately.

While staying at El Tovar Hotel, guests can admire views of Arizona's most magnificent landmark, the Grand Canyon, from several windows in the El Tovar Dining Room. Staying true to its rugged environment, the room reflects the beauty surrounding it, with touches of Oregon pine wooden beams and native stone walls. The global menu has of beauty all its own, infusing classic recipes with contemporary touches to appeal to the wordly clientele who've come for the other-wordly view.

SALTED CARAMEL PANNA COTTA

Recipe courtesy of
elements
Chef Beau MacMillan
Paradise Valley
480-667-2300

SERVES 8

MILK CHOCOLATE GANACHE

1/4 cup	cream
8 ounces	milk chocolate

SALTED CARAMEL SAUCE

2 cups	sugar
2 teaspoons	fleur de sel
2 cups	cream

SALTED CARAMEL PANNA COTTA

1 1/2 cup	milk
2 teaspoons	powdered gelatin
1 3/4 cup	cream
1 1/4 cup	salted caramel sauce- recipe above

1. In a double boiler, add cream and chocolate. Cook over medium heat until chocolate is melted. Carefully pour chocolate mixture into 8 glasses, 6 ounces in size. Place in refrigerator to cool.

2. Place sugar and salt in a separate saucepan, and cook on medium high heat, stirring frequently until the mixture turns dark amber in color. In a separate pot, bring cream to a boil and add amber colored caramel.

3. Place 1 cup milk in a bowl; sprinkle in gelatin, let set for 10 minutes.

4. Heat cream and add gelatin mixture. Blend and add salted caramel sauce. Pour equal amounts into glasses on top of milk chocolate. Serve immediately.

Nestled on the side of Camelback Mountain—where stunning views have made it a romantic destination—Sanctuary on Camelback Mountain opened in 2001 in what was once John Gardiner's tennis ranch. At its signature fine dining restaurant, elements, executive chef Beau MacMillan (a celebrated Food Network star) creates farm-fresh American cuisine with an Asian accent. "The breathtaking views of the desert and the striking colors of Arizona sunsets are carried out with a colorful presentation of our food," says MacMillan. His mouthwatering panna cotta, detailed here, is a favorite. "It takes a traditional dessert and makes it something really special," he says. "It is a dessert that everyone loves—not too sweet, not too salty."

BEEF CHILE NEGRO

Recipe courtesy of
Elote Cafe
Chef Jeff Smedstad
Sedona
928-203-0105

"I didn't choose Sedona; Sedona chose me," says Chef-owner Jeff Smedstad, whose creative riffs on regional Mexican food classics had earned him a following in Phoenix long before he moved to Red Rock country in 2006. From his colorful, second-floor café, this longhaired, late-model hippie cranks out seasonal dishes using thousands of pounds of local product each year— including tomatoes, chilies and goat cheese from Sedona and the Verde Valley. Living la vida locavore comes naturally to Smedstad, as does creating soul-satisfying dishes such as this one.

SERVES 8

2 pounds	boneless beef short ribs
	Salt and pepper to taste
1 cup	diced carrots
1 cup	diced onion
1 cup	celery
4 cups	low salt beef stock
1 pound	thick bacon, cooked crispy

FOR CHILE NEGRO SAUCE

1 tablespoon	olive oil
2 cups	chopped onion
1 cup	chopped garlic
4	pasilla chiles, seeded and chopped
4 cups	beef stock
1/8 teaspoon	cumin
1/4 teaspoon	allspice
1/2 teaspoon	oregano
1 teaspoon	salt
1/4 teaspoon	black pepper

FOR NEGRO AIOLI

3	egg yolks
4	garlic cloves
1 tablespoon	sherry vinegar
1 tablespoon	Worcestershire
2 1/4 teaspoon	ground chile negro
1 1/2 teaspoon	ground chipotle chile
1 tablespoon	Cholula sauce
1 1/2 teaspoons	salt
1/2 teaspoon	pepper
3/4 teaspoon	sugar
1 1/2 teaspoon	Mexican oregano
1 tablespoon	lime juice
2 cups	olive oil

1. Cut beef into 2-inch cubes. Season with salt and pepper. Cover and allow to rest at least 2 hours, preferably overnight, in the refrigerator.

2. Heat oven to 325 degrees. Also, heat a Dutch oven on medium high heat. Add oil and when hot add beef in small batches. Cook until beef is browned on all sides. Remove beef and reserve

3. In same pan, add carrots, onions and celery, sauté until al dente, about 5 minutes. Add stock and cover Dutch oven. Bake for 3 hours.

4. To make negro sauce, heat large skillet on medium heat. Add oil, and when hot add onion, garlic, and chilies. Sauté 5-7 minutes, being careful not to burn the garlic, then add remaining ingredients and simmer until soft, about 5 minutes. Allow to cool slightly, then puree in a blender or food processor.

5. To make aioli, all ingredients except oil into a blender. Puree until smooth. With blender running at medium speed, add oil in a slow, thin stream until completely incorporated.

6. Divide among 4 plates, top with 2 teaspoons of aioli, crunchy raw vegetables and the bacon.

APPLE TARTE TATIN

Recipe courtesy of
Essence Bakery
Chef Eugenia Theodosopoulos
Tempe
480-966-2745

On a trip to Colorado, where they discovered many restaurants serving naturally raised meats and organic ingredients, Essence owners Eugenia Theodosopoulos and Gilles Combes saw an opportunity to channel their passions for organic food and environmentally friendly business practices into a charming cafe and bakery back home in Arizona. Open since 2008, their busy Tempe location highlights seasonal produce and other sustainable, locally sourced ingredients, all served up with Gallic flair derived from Theodosopoulos' years of working with distinguished chefs in France. Here, she shares a comforting version of a timeless French dessert.

SERVES 8

8 medium or 6 large	apples, fuji or granny smith or combo of both
1 cup	sugar
6 tablespoon	water
1/2 stick	unsalted butter or 1/4 cup at room temperature – cut into 8 pieces
1 sheet	raw puff pastry or pie dough
	Chantilly or crème fraiche for garnish

1. Preheat oven to 350 degrees. Peel and core apples. Slice apples into thin concentric circles and making sure to keep shape of apple. Combine sugar and water in saucepan. Stir with whisk to combine, remove whisk and do not stir anymore with this whisk. Cook sugar and water over medium high heat, continuing to brush down sides of pan with wet pastry brush to avoid sugar from crystallizing. Cook caramel to deep amber color. Remove from heat and add butter with a clean whisk, piece by piece, to make a thick caramel. Pour into 8 – 3-inch high large muffin pans or 8-inch cake pan with 3-inch sides.

2. Add thinly sliced apples to caramel pressing down into caramel. Completely fill to brim with as many apples as possible. Bake in oven for total of 1 1/2 hours removing from oven to pat down apples every 30 minutes. Allow to cool 30 minutes for small individual tartes or 1 hour for 1 large tarte.

3. Roll puff pastry or pie dough to little larger circles than tartes. Poke with fork. If using puff then cover and bake with a rack to avoid puff from rising too much. Bake until lightly golden brown. Place over cooled apple tartes and invert onto cooked pastry rounds. Serve at room temperature or gently reheat at 350 for about 10 minutes. Served with crème Chantilly or crème fraiche.

SWEET POTATO CHILAQUILES

Recipe courtesy of
Feast
Chef Doug Levy
Tucson
520-326-9363

SERVES 8-10

1	small onion
1 1/2 cups	sour cream
1/2 cup	whole milk
	Vegetable oil for frying
12	corn tortillas
1 1/2 cups	vegetable stock
8	tomatillos, husked, rinsed, and diced
2	jalapeños, seeded and chopped
1	garlic clove, chopped
1/2 cup	chopped fresh cilantro leaves
1	large sweet potato, about 3/4 pound, peeled and sliced 1/4-inch thick
	Olive oil for coating
	Salt and pepper to taste
1 tablespoon	vegetable shortening or vegetable oil
1/2 cup	grated Monterey Jack cheese
2	poblano chiles, roasted, peeled, seeded and diced
1	small red onion, shaved
1/4 cup	lemon juice

1. Chop the onion coarsely and set aside. In a mixing bowl, whisk the sour cream and milk together.

2. In a large skillet, pour enough vegetable oil to come 1/4 inch up the sides. Heat the oil over medium heat until a drop of water sizzles. Fry the tortillas, 1 at a time, until crisp, about 1 minute. If needed, continue adding oil.

3. Place the stock in a saucepan and bring to a boil. Add the tomatillos and cook until tender, about 6 minutes. Remove tomatillos and reserve stock. Place the tomatillos, jalapeños, chopped onion, garlic and cilantro in a blender or food processor and blend until smooth. Season with salt and pepper.

4. In a large skillet over medium heat, heat the vegetable shortening. Pour in the tomatillo mixture and stir constantly for about 5 minutes, until thick and dark. Add the reserved stock and bring to a boil. Reduce the heat and simmer for 8-10 minutes or until sauce is thick enough to coat the back of a spoon

5. Preheat the oven to 350 degrees. Lightly oil and season the sweet potatoes slice with salt and pepper. Place on a baking sheet and roast until just tender, about 15-18 minutes. Remove to a refrigerator to stop the cooking process.

6. Line an 8-inch square baking pan with 3 tortillas, broken up to allow them to cover the bottom. Pour 1/4 tomatillo sauce on top, and pour 1/4 sour cream-milk mixture on top of the sauce. Top with 1/4 cheese, and place 1/3 of the poblanos and sweet potatoes over the cheese. Repeat this process with the remaining tortillas, sauce, sour cream mixture, and cheese. The top layer will not have poblanos or sweet potato. Meanwhile, toss the shaved red onion in the lemon juice and marinate.

7. Cover the baking pan with plastic film and then aluminum foil and bake for 30 minutes, or until the cheese is melted and bubbly. Remove the film and foil, cut and serve. Garnish with the pickled red onion and serve.

Originally opened in 2001 as an upscale take-out counter, Feast has evolved into an award-winning sit-down restaurant highlighted by its farm-fresh menu. In fact, the menu, which changes every month, showcases ingredients fresh-plucked from the on-site herb, vegetable and fruit gardens. Led by Chef-owner Doug Levy, Feast's globe-straddling selections range from Mediterranean and Southeast Asian fare, to more traditional South-western flavors such as this bold, savory sweet-potato chilaquiles entrée. Most important, Levy says, Feast's casual and welcoming atmosphere is a reflection of "Arizona's more relaxed pace and way of life."

FnB BROCCOLI

Recipe courtesy of
FnB
Chef Charleen Badman
Scottsdale

Referencing industry lingo for "food and beverage," front-of-the-house vet Pavle Milic teamed up with Chef Charleen Badman to open a buzzy urban "gin joint" along Stetson Drive's restaurant row in late 2009, and quickly earned praise from Food + Wine *magazine for Badman's comforting contemporary American cuisine and Milic's pioneering Arizona wine list. Badman's close relationships with local farmers are evident in the parade of luscious, seasonal vegetable side dishes that compete with entrees for diners' attention. Her grilled broccoli recipe has something of a cult following for its citrusy, smoky allure.*

SERVES 4

2 cloves	garlic, peeled and finely chopped
	Pinch of salt
2	egg yolks
3/4 cup	blended oil, a combination of canola and extra virgin
1/4 cup	extra virgin
zest and juice of 1	tangerine or Meyer lemon
1/4 teaspoon	freshly ground pepper
1 teaspoon	water
2 heads	broccoli heads
2 tablespoons	sambal
1/4 cup	extra virgin olive oil
1/2 teaspoon	sea salt
1/4 teaspoon	freshly ground pepper
1/2 cup	toasted, salted pistachio pieces

1. To make aioli, place garlic, salt and egg yolks in a mixing bowl with the whisk attachment. Mix until well incorporated. Slowly dribble the blended oil into the yolk mixture. As the yolk absorbs the oil, the sauce will begin to thicken. When completely blended, add extra virgin olive oil, zest, citrus juice and pepper. Blend well, and add water. Mix again and add salt to taste.

2. Trim leaves from broccoli. Trim the base and peel the stalk with a peeler. If the stalks are thick, cut them lengthways in half or quarters to produce thinner stalks. Bring a pot of salted water to boil. Blanch broccoli for about 3 minutes or until tender, but still firm to touch. Drain in colander, rinse well with cold water and let dry, stalk end up to remove as much water from the floret as possible.

3. In a medium sized bowl, add sambal, oil, salt and pepper. Whisk until combined. Toss broccoli until evenly coated with sambal mixture. Prepare a hot fire for grilling. Oil the grill well to avoid sticking. Place broccoli on grill. Grill on both sides for 3 minutes. Place aioli on platter or four individual plates. Place broccoli on aioli and sprinkle with pistachio pieces.

"EL TEJANO" BURRITO

SERVES 2

1/4 cup	chorizo, optional
1/2 cup	refried beans
1 cup	tomatillo salsa
1/2 cup	sharp cheddar, grated
2 tablespoons	diced cilantro
2	small flour tortillas

1. Heat sauté pan on medium and add chorizo. Sauté, stirring often, until chorizo is cooked, about 5 minutes. While cooking chorizo, heat tortillas on a grill or in the oven. When done, set on a flat surface and divide beans equally, spreading from the center to 2 inches from the edges. Next, add the tomatillo salsa and cheese. Remove chorizo from pan, drain and place equal amounts in the center of the tortilla.

2. Fold the left and right sides of the tortilla towards the center. Then fold one edge just past the center of where the pork sits. Finish rolling into a cylinder. Place on broiling tray. Heat broiler and place rolls seam side down 6-inches away from heat. Toast 1-2 minutes and serve.

Recipe courtesy of
Gallo Blanco
Chef Doug Robson
Phoenix
602-274-4774

While Gallo Blanco Chef-owner Doug Robson draws much inspiration from his native Mexico City to serve a contemporary, upbeat take on Mexican street food at his Clarendon Hotel hangout, he says he chose to focus on Sonoran cooking for his cookbook submission. Intrigued by small Arizona towns such as Patagonia, Greer, Nogales and Willcox, Robson says he's fascinated by how different people find common ground in protecting their Latin heritage, regardless of which side of the border they live on. Robson's hearty burrito recipe reflects his commitment to supporting local food sources, and ultimately, doing business with one's neighbor as much as possible.

KILLER CHOCOLATE CAKE

Recipe courtesy of
Garden Café
Chef Debbie Gwen
Yuma
928-783-1491

If you can't spot the Garden Café from the street, don't fret. Follow the posted wooden signs until you come across a wonderful rainbow-colored awning shading the outdoor patio where guests relax in a blooming garden and listen to birds chirp. Take a trip to the café for their Sunday brunch buffet, piled high with breakfast favorites like quiche, Swedish pancakes, and fluffy scrambled eggs. On any other day, ask for a bowl of their famous tortilla soup, served hot with tortilla chips, avocados, onions and cheese.

MAKES ONE 9X13 CAKE

CAKE

3 cups	hot water, not boiling, just hot out of the tap
3 sticks	butter
2 1/4 cups	granulated sugar
3	eggs
2 tablespoons	vanilla
3 cups	all-purpose white flour
3 teaspoons	baking powder
3 teaspoons	baking soda
1 cup	Hershey's unsweetened dry cocoa

FROSTING

6 ounces	cream cheese
1/4 cup	butter
2 teaspoons	vanilla
3 cups	powdered sugar

1. Heat the water and butter until they are mixed. Set the mixture aside.

2. Beat together sugar, eggs, vanilla. Combine butter/water mixture with sugar eggs and vanilla mixture.

3. Combine flour, baking powder, baking soda, cocoa together into a bowl. Fold the liquid mixture into the dry mixture until thoroughly mixed.

4. Bake at 350 degrees for 45 minutes. Check with toothpick to see if it's solid. Let cake cool.

5. For frosting, whip cream cheese and butter together and fold in vanilla and powdered sugar until thoroughly mixed.

RACK OF LAMB
WITH CORIANDER CRUST
SERVES 4-6

Recipe courtesy of
Garland's Oak Creek Lodge
Chef Amanda Stine
Sedona
928-282-3343

MARINADE

2 tablespoons	coriander seeds
2 tablespoons	coarse black pepper
6	garlic cloves, chopped
4	green onions
3/4 cup	lemon juice
1 1/4 cups	olive oil
2 tablespoons	salt
2 tablespoons	sugar
8	small New Zealand or Australian lamb racks, French cut (ask butcher to cut)

CORIANDER CRUST

1/3 cup	coriander seeds
1 tablespoon	mustard seeds
1/2 cup	cilantro, chopped
1/2 cup	Italian parsley, chopped
1/4 cup	fresh sage, chopped
1/4 cup	fine dry breadcrumbs or panko
1 teaspoon	salt

1. Combine seeds, pepper, garlic, onions, juice, oil, salt and sugar in blender and process until smooth. Transfer to glass or plastic or non-reactive metal dish large enough to hold lamb racks. Trim extra fat and silver skin, or white membrane covering meat, off the racks. Place racks meat side down in the marinade. The bones can be sticking out of marinade. Set aside for 30-60 minutes

2. For crust, toast coriander and musturd seeds in a dry skillet on medium heat, stirring freqently, until fragrant, about 3-5 minutes. Remove and crush seeds in a spice grinder just enough to break them up, not grind into powder. Mix with herbs and bread crumbs, set aside.

3. Preheat oven to 350 degrees. Next, heat grill to medium heat, or heat cast iron skillet or grill pan over medium high. Remove racks from the marinade and drain very well. Lightly oil the grill or pan. Lay racks meat side down on the heat, and sear for 2 minutes. Remove racks to roasting or sheet pan, meat side up. Sprinkle and press about 1 to 2 tablespoons of the crust mixture over the lamb meat, covering lightly. Place pan in upper rack of oven and roast for 10 to 15 minutes, depending on preference. Serve on warm plates.

Lush with gardens, flowers and fruit trees, this idyllic spot has been a lodge, in one form or another, since the late '20s — first as a fried-chicken stopover for Jerome's miners, who fished the creek on Sundays, and later after the Garland family bought the property in 1972, as a relaxing getaway for frazzled city folks. Guests who stay in the rustic "unplugged" cabins are automatically treated to Chef Amanda Stine's hearty breakfasts and simple yet sophisticated four-course dinners. Non-guests who call in advance might land a few extra seats at one of the shared tables.

KOTOPITA

Recipe courtesy of
Greekfest
Chef Tony Makridis
Phoenix
602-265-2990

Fusing tradition with innovation, Greekfest's authentic Greek/ Mediterranean cuisine provides guests with a unique taste of Greece in a setting that transports them back to the charm of the Aegean. Greekfest's trademark is the spirited reinvention of island cuisine, fusing wild greens, fruits, savory meats and home-grown herbs to achieve spectacular and unexpected flavors. Come and relax, converse and celebrate the fine Greek cuisine that we they have been perfecting now for 33 years in business. Opa!

SERVES 4

1	medium onion, chopped
4	garlic cloves, chopped
4	chicken breasts, roasted
2 cups	pistachios, chopped
2 cups	Kasseri cheese, grated
2 cups	Kefalotyri cheese, grated
2 tablespoons	orange zest, chopped
2 cups	extra virgin olive oil
1-pound	package phyllo pastry
	Salt and pepper, to taste
2 teaspoons	ground nutmeg
1 cup	sweet basil, chopped
2	eggs beaten (optional)

1. Roast chicken at 350 degrees for 1/2 hour. When cooled down, skin, debone and chop chicken.

2. Sauté onions and garlic in one cup of olive oil until translucent.

3. In a bowl, add the chicken, onions, pistachios, orange zest, Kasseri and Kefalotyri cheeses, salt and pepper, nutmeg, sweet basil and beaten eggs. Mix well.

4. Open phyllo and cut in half lengthwise. Take one sheet of phyllo and fold in half lengthwise, brush with olive oil and add a small spoonful of the mix and fold in a triangle.

5. When mix is finished, arrange on a cookie sheet and brush oil on the top. Bake in preheated oven, 400 degrees for 10 minutes or until golden.

OLIVE-ROAST SEA BASS
"IN THE STYLE OF NICOISE"

SERVES 4

Recipe courtesy of
Heirloom
Chef Michael DeMaria
Scottsdale

After a successful run creating one of North Scottsdale's finest Italian restaurants, Michael's at the Citadel, where Chef/owner Michael DeMaria taught culinarians and foodies alike the art of Italian cooking, he returned in 2009 with Heirloom, an American restaurant. Set under the twinkling lights of Market Street at DC Ranch, Heirloom is DeMaria's playground, operating as a pop-up restaurant hosting themed dinners and cooking classes for the desert-dwellers living in the scenic foothills of Pinnacle Peak.

SEA BASS
	Olive oil for searing
4	sea bass fillets (about 5 ounces each)
2 tablespoons	black olive tapenade
Pinch	Kosher salt
	Black pepper, to taste

THE POTATOES
6	Russet potatoes
1/4 cup	unsalted butter
1 tablespoon	garlic
	Kosher salt (to taste)
	Cracked black pepper (to taste)
1 tablespoon	chives, chopped
1/4 cup	half n' half, warm and only if needed

"NIÇOISE" VEGETABLES
2	whole red tomatoes, concassé
1 cup	sliced and blanched haricot verts

ANCHOVY BUTTER
1/4 cup	unsalted butter, whipped
1 teaspoon	anchovy, chopped fine
1 teaspoon	capers, chopped fine
1 teaspoon	parsley, chopped
1 teaspoon	garlic, chopped
1 teaspoon	shallots, chopped
	Salt and pepper to taste

TOMATO VINAIGRETTE
8	Roma tomatoes
2 tablespoons	chopped shallots
2 tablespoons	chopped garlic
1 tablespoon	diced olives
2 tablespoons	chopped parsley
1 tablespoon	dry oregano
1/2 cup	red wine vinegar
1 cup	olive oil
	Salt and pepper to taste

FINAL GARNISH
Italian parsley sprigs
Basil oil as needed

PREPARE THE SEA BASS:

1. Preheat oven to 375 degrees. Heat a non-stick skillet on high heat. Add oil. Place fish in skillet; add tapenade, salt and pepper. Cook until the flesh begins to look cooked around the sides, about 1-2 minutes. Turn fish and place pan in a 375 degree oven for 3 to 6 minutes, depending on desired doneness. Set aside.

2. Bring salted pot of water to about 200 degrees. Cut potatoes into 2-inch chunks and place them into hot water. Keep the temperature just before a rolling boil and cook until fork tender, about 10 minutes. Drain potatoes through a colander. Let sit until totally dry. Empty potatoes into a mixing bowl. Add butter and mix on Number 1 speed until all incorporated. Add salt, pepper, horseradish and whip until smooth on speed Number 2 speed for 3 minutes. Stop and scrape all sides. Whip on speed Number 3 speed for 2 more minutes. Adjust with salt and pepper. Scoop all potatoes out into a new bowl and cover with plastic wrap. When serving, fold in the chopped chives and serve.

Note: The half n' half should be kept warm and only add when the mashers are starchy. Fold in a little when necessary.

3. Bring pot of salted water to boil. Core tomatoes by making an "X" on the top with paring knife. Add to boiling water and allow to cook for 10 to 20 seconds.

Note: This time can be longer or shorter depending on the ripeness of tomatoes. When skin starts to peel back, remove tomatoes from boiling water and shock it in ice-cold water. Leave it in cold water until tomatoes are cold. The skin should slip right off. Using paring knife, remove all skin and place tomato on paper towel-lined pan to absorb all excess liquid.

4. Snip the woody tip off the vert stem. Use blanch and shock technique used for tomatoes. Allow to cool slightly then slice 1/4 inch thick slices of green bean. Reserve.

5. For anchovy butter, place whipped butter in a mixing bowl until soft. Next, add remaining ingredients to taste. Add to sauté pan on medium high heat. When melted, sauté 2 tomatoes and verts in butter until hot, about 3-4 minutes. Set aside and keep warm.

6. To prepare vinaigrette, place whole tomatoes in the bowl of a food processor fitted with metal blade. Puree tomatoes until smooth and then strain through fine mesh sieve; discard solids. Add chopped shallots, minced garlic, olives, herbs and vinegar to tomato puree. Slowly whisk in oil until you reach the desired consistency and flavor. Season with salt and pepper.

7. Using a spoon, Quenelle-scoop or simply scoop enough mashed potatoes to feed 4 in center of plate. Place fish on top of potatoes. Now spoon around vinaigrette and spoon vegetables over top. Add parsley sprigs and drizzle basil oil around plate.

Note: Quenelle is a three-sided delicate shape that takes time to master. It is made by twisting two spoons together working a three-sided shape.

PRUNE AND STAR ANISE BRAISED LAMB SHANK

WITH TOASTED CINNAMON FARRO RISOTTO, SMOKED KALE, SLIVERED ALMONDS AND ROASTED BUTTERNUT SQUASH-CHORIZO VINAIGRETTE

Recipe courtesy of
House of Tricks
Chef Kelly Eugene Fletcher
Tempe
480-968-1114

SERVES 4

4	lamb hind shanks
1/4 cup	duck fat (or canola oil)
1	large yellow onion, peeled and julienned
1	carrot, peeled and sliced into 1/2-inch rounds
1/2	leek, white part only, rinsed well and julienned
3	cloves of garlic, whole, peeled
2 cups	ruby port
2 cups	red wine
1/2	ginger root, peeled
1 cup	prunes
1/2 cup	slivered almonds
1/2	cinnamon stick
2	cloves
8	star anises
2 cups	beef stock
	Peel from 1/2 an orange, pith removed

FARRO RISOTTO

2 cups	farro
8 cups	chicken stock
1 teaspoon	cinnamon
4 tablespoons	butter
1/2 cup	minced shallot
1 cup	white wine
4 tablespoons	Parmesan

BUTTERNUT SQUASH-CHORIZO VINAIGRETTE

1/2	butternut squash
1/3 cup	chorizo
1	shallot, minced
3	cloves of garlic, minced
1 tablespoon	minced chive
1/4 cup	white balsamic
1/2 cup	extra virgin olive oil

Photo: John Ormond

1. Preheat oven to 350 degrees. Season the lamb with salt and pepper and melt the duck fat or canola oil in a large stock pot and sear the lamb on all sides until golden brown. Add the onions, carrots, leeks and garlic and cook for another 5 minutes. Add the red wine and port and simmer for another 5 minutes. Add all other ingredients, cover tightly with foil and roast for about 3 hours, or until the lamb is tender on the bone.

2. Soak the farro in cold water for 20 minutes. Meanwhile, heat chicken stock with cinnamon in a stockpot. In a separate saucepan over medium heat, melt the butter, add shallots and sauté until translucent, about 5 minutes. Add the white wine and strained off farro. Sauté 2 minutes. Add the chicken stock one cup at a time and simmer until the liquid is absorbed, stirring often, about 14 minutes. Stir in the parmesan and season with salt and pepper.

3. Butternut Squash-Chorizo Vinaigrette: Peel and cut the squash into 1/4-inch dice, lightly coat in oil and season with salt and pepper and roast in a 350 degree oven until fork tender. Cool to room temperature. Cook the chorizo in a sauté pan and cool to room temperature. In a large bowl, whisk in all other ingredients with the squash and chorizo. Serve lamb, farro and squash dishes warm.

Strolling under mature trees through the lush, magical patio leading up to House of Tricks, diners find it hard to believe that the 1920's cottage serving as the restaurant's main dining room was a run-down print shop that required a seven-month remodel before Robert and Robin Trick opened for business in 1987. Likewise, the historic adobe brick structure next door, which was beautifully restored and turned into additional dining rooms, seems just as elegant as it must've looked when it was built in 1903. To complement the refined atmosphere, chef Kelly Eugene Fletcher creates contemporary American cuisine that respects tradition while staying progressive. And in anticipation of the cooler temperatures that make Arizona winters worth the wait, he presents this luscious lamb shank recipe as an example of the restaurant's dynamic cuisine.

WARM CHOCOLATE CAKE

Recipe courtesy of
J&G Steakhouse
Chef Jacques Qualin
Scottsdale
480-214-8000

SERVES 4

1 stick (4 ounces)	unsalted butter
6 ounces	bittersweet chocolate, preferably Valrhona
2	eggs
2	egg yolks
1/4 cup	sugar
	Pinch of salt
2 tablespoons	all-purpose flour

1. Preheat the oven to 450 degrees. Butter and lightly flour four 6-ounce ramekins. Tap out the excess flour. Set the ramekins on a baking sheet.

2. In a double boiler, over simmering water, melt the butter with the chocolate. In a medium bowl, beat the eggs with the egg yolks, sugar and salt at high speed until thickened and pale.

3. Whisk the chocolate until smooth. Quickly fold it into the egg mixture along with the flour. Spoon the batter into the prepared ramekins and bake for 12 minutes, or until the sides of the cakes are firm but the centers are soft. Let the cakes cool in the ramekins for 1 minute, then cover each with an inverted dessert plate. Carefully turn each one over, let stand for 10 seconds and then unmold. Serve immediately.

The batter can be refrigerated for several hours; bring to room temperature before baking.

If the Greek gods had stumbled upon Camelback Mountain before Mount Olympus, J&G Steakhouse very well may have been their dining room. As such, it's no surprise that the sprawling fifth-floor space perched atop one of the Valley's premier resorts, The Phoenician, attracted famed chef Jean-Georges Vongerichten as the site for his latest creation. With floor to ceiling windows and a patio that offers the best views of the sprawling Arizona landscape, J&G is a contemporary steakhouse designed by famed architect David Rockwell. At the helm in the kitchen is chef de cuisine Jacques Qualin, who cranks out classics. Featuring a bevy of bone-in steaks, a global selection of seafood, seasonal sides sourced from local farmers, and farm-to-cocktail libations, the palatable strokes of genius from a chef as mystical as his culinary creations have made waves in a town tantalized by meat and potatoes.

EL PRESIDIO PAN-FRIED CHICKEN

Recipe courtesy of
Janos and J Bar
Chef Janos Wilder
Tucson
520-615-6100

If you want to broaden your gastronomical horizons in Tucson, Janos is your best bet. The James Beard Award-winning Chef Janos Wilder is a culinary mastermind, using traditional and exotic ingredients in unconventional presentations. His brilliance is demonstrated through a blend of French and Southwestern styles, which manifests into such creations as a Trilogy of Blue Corn Fritters made with duck confit, pork belly, pickled watermelon and prickly pear syrup; Braised Pork Belly with Tohono O'odham H:al Squash; and Sassafras and Cocoa-dusted Venison Ibarra.

SERVES 5+

1 1/4 pounds	boneless, skinless breasts
1	egg white
1	Anaheim chili, peeled, seeded and diced
1 cup	grated cheddar cheese
1	tomato, diced
1/2 bunch	scallions, finely diced
1 tablespoon	fresh garlic, finely chopped
1/2 cup	fresh cilantro, coarsely chopped
1/3 cup	heavy cream
	Salt and pepper to taste

BREADING

3 cups	all-purpose flour
1 cup	milk
4 cups	coarse bread crumbs
	Vegetable oil for frying

1. Preheat oven to 350 degrees. Cut chicken breasts into chunks and quickly process in a food processor along with egg whites. Do not puree: chicken should be fairly coarse.

2. Fold in chili, cheese, tomatoes, scallions, garlic, chopped cilantro, cream, season with salt and pepper.

3. Shape mixture into patties about 3/4 inch thick weighing 6 1/2 ounces. Set out individual containers of flour, milk and bread crumbs. Dust with flour, dip in milk and coat with bread crumbs, handling carefully so that patties maintain their shape.

4. Heat 1/4 inch oil in a sauté pan. Add patties and fry until golden-brown, turning once. Finish in oven, about 7 minutes.

JOE'S REAL ST. LOUIS CUT SPARE RIBS

SERVES 4

Recipe courtesy of
Joe's Real BBQ
Chef Joseph Johnston
Gilbert
480-503-3805

	Full slab of ribs, peeled
2 cups	granulated brown sugar
1 cup	granulated white sugar
2 tablespoons	granulated garlic
1 tablespoon	black pepper
2 teaspoons	cayenne pepper
2 teaspoons	seasoning salt
1 teaspoon	coriander
2 tablespoons	dried oregano
1 tablespoon	chili powder

1. Combine all dry ingredients in a bowl and liberally rub the entire slab of ribs before smoking.

2. To cook the ribs, preheat the oven to 210 degrees. Place in roasting pan and cover with foil. Roast for 3 1/2 to 4 hours, or until the meat pulls away from the bone. If you are using a grill, try to use indirect heat over favorite wood chips about 3 hours. Always cook ribs meat side up and check the ribs after two hours.

After founding the successful Coffee Plantation, a local coffeehouse chain which they operated for seven years and then sold, Joe Johnston and Tim Peelen helped their former company roll out nearly 20 new stores in Texas—which ended up being the perfect opportunity to start researching barbecue for their new restaurant. They renovated a handsome 1929 building right in the middle of Downtown Gilbert that was originally a Safeway Pay'n'Takit, creating a 1940s-inspired atmosphere with framed vintage copies of Arizona Highways, *a 1948 John Deere tractor in the middle of the dining room and a mural titled "The Fruit of Our Labor," which celebrates the area's agricultural heritage. Since opening day in 1998, their flavorful, "low and slow" smoked ribs continue to be a menu highlight.*

BAKLAVA-WRAPPED BRIE
WITH ORANGE CARDAMOM HONEY

SERVES 16-20

Recipe courtesy of
Josephine's Modern American Bistro
*Owner and Chef
Tony Cosentino
Flagstaff
928-779-3400*

The lovely red-stone building that houses Josephine's was once the distinguished home of the John Milton Clarke family. And although it's been transformed into a cozy modern American bistro with a decidedly eclectic bent, this lovely old place still evokes home, thanks to two fireplaces and an intimate patio. In the kitchen, Chef Tony Cosentino brings together global ingredients and classic technique to create a fine dining experience that reflects a modern American sensibility. Baklava-wrapped Brie, drizzled with orange-cardamom honey, represents his approach perfectly. It's sophisticated but very approachable.

1	orange
1 pound	honey
1/2 tablespoon	cardamom whole seeds
6 sheets	phyllo
	Melted butter or spray
1/2 cup	pistachios, grounded
2 pounds	Brie
	Crackers or crostini for serving

1. Peel the very outside of the orange, leaving the pith on the orange. Place the honey, juice from the orange, cardamom and peel in a saucepan. Simmer on low heat until the mixture is the consistency of honey. Strain seeds out and set aside. Can be prepared days in advance

2. Thaw phyllo. If it dries out quickly, cover with wet, drained towel. Lay a sheet of phyllo on counter. Brush with melted butter or spray liberally. Place another layer of phyllo directly over the first, and butter again. Sprinkle light layer of ground pistachios. Repeat 3 times for a total of 6 layers. Don't worry if some of the layers are not perfect.

3. Preheat oven to 400 degrees. Place Brie in center of phyllo and wrap, overlapping the phyllo. Flip the wrapped Brie over onto a sheet pan and brush top with butter.

4. Bake Brie at 400 degrees for 10 to 15 minutes, until golden brown. Place on decorative platter and top with the honey and remaining pistachios. Serve with crackers or crostini.

TEQUILA CHICKEN

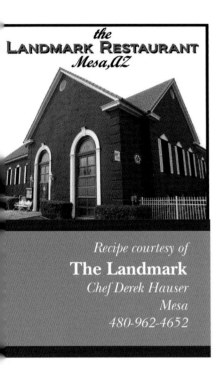

LANDMARK RESTAURANT
the
Mesa, AZ

Recipe courtesy of
The Landmark
Chef Derek Hauser
Mesa
480-962-4652

Originally built as a Mormon church in the early 1900s, this lovely building has been home to The Landmark Restaurant in Mesa for the past 30 years. The Landmark, owned by Don and Candy Ellis, offers much more than Midwestern, home-style cooking. In recent years, the couple has made it a point to branch out by enlisting Chef Derek Hauser to create dishes such as tequila chicken, offering them a taste unlike any other. The Landmark's several private rooms and catering services create the perfect place to host weddings, banquets and private parties.

SERVES 2

SEASONED FLOUR

1 1/2 cup	flour
1 tablespoon	salt
1 tablespoon	garlic salt
1 tablespoon	black pepper
1/2 tablespoon	white pepper

2	chicken breasts, about 6-8 ounces each, halved, pounded
2 tablespoons	olive oil
2 slivers	each red, yellow and green bell peppers
3	button mushrooms, sliced
1/2 cup	red onion slices
3	slices pickled jalapeño
1/4 cup	chicken stock
4 tablespoons	tequila
1/4 cup	heavy cream

CHEESE MIX

2 tablespoons	shredded cheddar cheese
1 tablespoon	bacon bits
1 tablespoon	diced green onion

1. For seasoned flour, mix all ingredients together in a large mixing bowl and set aside.

2. Pound chicken breasts and cut into 2 pieces, coat with flour mixture and heat sauté pan on medium high heat. Add olive oil, and when hot, add chicken breast. Sauté 3–4 minutes, or until golden brown. Turn and add peppers, mushrooms, red onion and jalapeños. Sauté for 1–2 minutes. Add chicken stock and tequila. Reduce heat to medium low and simmer to reduce and thicken.

3. Prepare cheese mix in small bowl. After stock and tequila have reduced by almost half, add heavy cream and continue to simmer and reduce for another 5-7 minutes. Reduce heat to low and add cheese mix and heat until creamy and cheese has melted. Transfer to plate and serve.

MENUDO

SERVES 8-10

10 pounds	beef tripe, trimmed of fat
3 to 4 gallons	water
4 pounds	dry white hominy
1/2 cup	fresh garlic
2	medium yellow onions

1. Trim fat off beef tripe and cut into small squares about 2 to 4 inches or preference. Then, soak beef tripe in lemon and salt solution for about a half hour to wash odor and bleach meat.

2. Place beef tripe and water in a 5-gallon pot. Cook on medium heat for about 2 hours. More time may be needed due to texture preference. Add water as needed.

3. After 2 hours or so, add fresh garlic and 2 peeled medium yellow onions, cut in half. Add dry hominy and cook for an additional hour or until hominy "pops". Add water as needed. After 45 minutes cooking, add salt to taste.

4. Remove from heat and let Menudo stand for a half hour to let flavors set. Divide up amongst bowls and serve.

Recipe courtesy of
La Perla Café
Joe Pompa, Owner
Clendale
623-939-7561

Joe Pompa (who claimed Geronimo shared his family tree) and his wife, Eva (who was born in Chihuahua), grew up in the Jerome-Clarkdale area, where he worked in the copper mines. The couple moved to Glendale and opened La Perla in 1946. With help from his children, grandchildren, nieces and nephews, Joe Jr. runs the place these days — still making fresh corn and flour tortillas, grinding chiles by stone and making fluffy chile rellenos the old-fashioned way. Local movers and shakers including John McCain, Jim Hensley and the Martori Brothers have all been frequent customers.

PORK CARNITAS

Recipe courtesy of
La Piñata
Chef Peter Bugarin
Phoenix
602-279-1763

In 1970, Peter Bugarin, along with his mother and father, opened La Piñata Restaurant to showcase their unique approach to the fried burrito, otherwise known as the chimichanga, and nearly 40 years later, La Piñata is still deemed "home of the chimichanga." The family claims their famous chimi was the first to be topped with sour cream, guacamole, tomatoes, onion and cheese. It comes filled with an array of stuffings including beans, green or red chile, ground beef, chicken or machaca.

SERVES 6

5 pounds	pork (butt or shoulder boneless)
1 tablespoon	salt
1/2 teaspoon	pepper
1 teaspoon	garlic powder
1/2 pound	canola, vegetable oil or pork lard
1/4 - 1/2	cup milk
	Squeeze of fresh orange
	Tortillas for serving

1. Cut pork into 4-by-4 chunks, cutting away as much fat as possible. Mix together salt, pepper and garlic powder. Rub mixture on all sides of pork.

2. In a deep Dutch oven, add oil and heat on medium-high and when oil begins to smoke, add pork. Sear on all sides in batches.

3. . Reduce heat to simmer and add all pork back to pot. Cover and cook for 1 hour, turning meat every 15, to 20 minutes.

4. After 1 hour, add milk, re-cover and continue to cook for 30-45 minutes. Remove meat to drain on paper towels.

5. While still hot, using 2 forks, shred pork, and if needed re-season with more salt, garlic or pepper. A squeeze of fresh orange juice finishes the dish. Serve with flour or corn tortillas.

BBQ BRAISED SHORT RIBS
GLAZED ROOT VEGETABLES AND HICKORY-SMOKED POLENTA

Recipe courtesy of
L'Auberge Restaurant
*Chef David Schmidt
Sedona
928-282-1661*

Tucked away in a tree-shaded canyon along the banks of burbling Oak Creek, this rustic but luxurious boutique resort boasts one of the most gorgeous settings in Northern Arizona. From spring to fall, there's no better place to be than the sun-dappled dining terrace perched at the water's edge. Executive Chef David Schmidt, who presides over the Mediterranean-inflected American menu, buys local and seasonal product, house-cures meats for his charcuterie board and forages hundreds of pounds of wild mushrooms every fall. He swears his short rib recipe "warms the belly and hits home with everyone."

SERVES 8

RIBS

2 pounds	bone-in short ribs
	Salt and pepper to taste
2 tablespoons	olive oil
2 stalks	celery, medium dice
2	peeled carrots, medium dice
1	onion, medium dice
3 tablespoons	tomato paste
2 cups	red wine
1 pint	beef stock
4 sprigs	thyme
3	cloves of peeled garlic
1	bay leaf

BBQ SAUCE

1 tablespoon	olive oil
5	Roma tomatoes, quartered
8	peaches, quartered and deseeded
1/2	onion, medium diced
3	cloves of whole garlic
1 cup	red wine
2 cups	pineapple juice
2 cups	tomato juice
5 sprigs	thyme
1 sprig	oregano
1	bay leaf

HICKORY SMOKED POLENTA

2 tablespoons	olive oil
1	medium onion, diced small
1 cup	polenta
2 sprigs	thyme
3 cups	beef stock
1/2 cup	milk
1 tablespoon	honey
	Powdered hickory smoke or liquid smoke to taste
	Salt and pepper to taste
1 tablespoon	unsalted butter

FOR GLAZED VEGETABLES

1 pound	favorite root vegetables such as carrots or turnips, cut into bite-size pieces
2 tablespoons	butter
	Beef broth for glazing
	Fresh herbs

1. Season beef short ribs liberally with salt and pepper. In a braising pan on medium heat, add olive oil, and just before the oil begins to smoke, add short ribs. Reduce heat to low. Slowly brown ribs on all sides. When done, remove short ribs and reserve.

2. Add celery, carrots and onions. Slowly cook until caramelized, about 15 to 20 minutes. Add tomato paste and cook for 1 minute.

3. Heat oven to 350 degrees. Add wine and reduce to the consistency of syrup. Add beef stock, thyme, garlic and bay leaf. Bring to a boil. Add short ribs to liquid. Remove from heat. Tightly wrap with aluminum foil. Cook for about 3 hours.

4. To make BBQ sauce, heat saucepot on medium heat. Add olive oil, and when hot, add onions and garlic. Sauté until soft, about 5 minutes. Add tomatoes and peaches. Cook till almost all liquid has evaporated from the tomatoes. Add wine, pineapple and tomato juices. Cook, stirring occasionally, until reduced by half, about 20 minutes. Carefully transfer to a blender and blend until smooth. Transfer sauce back to pot. Add herbs, garlic and bay leaf. Cook till flavors are incorporated, about 10 minutes. Salt and pepper to taste. Strain through a fine mesh strainer into a bowl. Cover and keep warm until ready to serve.

5. Meanwhile, to make polenta, heat heavy gauge sauce pot on medium heat. Add olive oil, and when hot, add onions and cook until translucent, about 5 minutes. Next, add polenta, herbs, stock and milk. Cook, stirring constantly, until polenta is cooked through. Add honey and remaining seasonings. Finish with butter.

6. For glazed vegetables, blanch in hot water and shock in ice cold water. Next, in a large sauté pan, add butter. When hot add vegetables and sauté for 5-8 minutes. Splash with beef broth and add fresh herbs. Sauté another 2 minutes and serve immediately.

TURKEY RELLENO SANDWICH

SERVES 2

2	eggs
1 cup	heavy cream for egg batter
1 tablespoon	canola oil for frying
10 ounces	thinly sliced roasted turkey breast
4 ounces	diced green chilies
1 tablespoon	water for steaming
4	thick slices, about 3/4-inch, sourdough bread
4 slices	pepper Jack cheese
	Salsa for serving

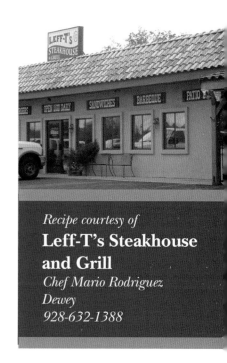

Recipe courtesy of
Leff-T's Steakhouse and Grill
Chef Mario Rodriguez
Dewey
928-632-1388

1. Whip together eggs and heavy cream; set aside. Heat frying pan or heavy skillet to medium heat, add canola oil.

2. In a small pan, place turkey and green chilies. Add 1 tablespoon water, cover and steam over medium heat until just hot.

3. Dip bread slices into egg/cream mixture. Place in a hot pan. Fry one side until golden, and turn over

4. Lay cheese slice on each piece of bread. Place hot turkey and green chili mixture on two bread slices. Cover with remaining two pieces of bread. Heat large sauté pan on medium high heat. Add sandwiches and cook until cheese melts and bread begins to crisp. Remove, slice in half and serve with your favorite fresh salsa.

This Western-styled steakhouse has become the perfect spot in Dewey to get dressed up for a night out or to just grab a bite to eat in your jeans. Slip into one of the red leather booths and enjoy a rack of Leff-T's famous Mesquite Smoked Baby Back Ribs, one of the large T-bone steaks served with a dollop of warm garlic butter, or pick from an array of good ol' hamburgers and sandwiches, such as this unique turkey relleno.

CALABACITAS

Recipe courtesy of
Lerua's Fine Mexican Foods
Chef Michael Hultquist
Tucson
520-624-0322

Tony Lerua and family started selling tamales from their home in 1922, moving the business in 1932 and again nine years later to the current location on Broadway. In the early '60s, Carmen Borgaro began leasing the space from Lerua and bought the business in 1964, maintaining the reputation he'd established for outstanding tamales. When Borgara's health began to fail in the '80s, her sons Mike and Brad Hultquist stepped in to help (Mike had spent years working at prestigious La Roca in Nogales), and the brothers finally bought the business in 1988. Lerua's comforting Mexican home-cooking is as popular as ever.

SERVES 4-6

1/2 cup	butter or margarine
1	medium onion, diced
6	fresh Italian (green) squash, quartered lengthwise and diced
2	Anaheim chiles, roasted, peeled and cut into strips
1/4 cup	vegetable broth
2	tomatoes quartered into wedges
2 cups	yellow corn (fresh or canned and drained)
	Garlic powder, to taste
	Salt, to taste
1 tablespoon	black pepper
	Grated cheese

1. Put butter in pan and cook onion for about 5 minutes until softened. Add squash, chiles and broth. Cook about 10-15 minutes until liquid has reduced. Add tomatoes and corn. Add garlic powder, salt and black pepper. Heat through and serve with grated cheese on top.

MEDALLIONS OF PORK
WITH RASPBERRY-CHIPOTLE SAUCE

Recipe courtesy of
Les Gourmettes
Chef Barbara Fenzl
Phoenix
602-240-6767

SERVES 2

1 tablespoon	unsalted butter
1	pork tenderloin, about 3/4 pound, cut into medallions
	Salt and freshly ground pepper to taste

SAUCE

1 tablespoon	finely chopped shallots
1	clove garlic, finely chopped
6 ounces	unsweetened frozen raspberries, thawed
1 tablespoon	sugar
1/2 cup	dry red wine
1 cup	chicken stock
1 tablespoon	adobo sauce from a can of chipotle chiles
1 tablespoon	butter
	Salt and freshly ground pepper to taste

1. Heat butter in a large skillet over medium heat. Season medallions with salt and pepper and brown meat on both sides, about 1 minute per side. Remove to a warm plate and set aside.

2. Add shallots and garlic to the pan in which the pork was sautéed and cook about 20 seconds. Add raspberries and sugar and cook, stirring, 30 seconds longer. Add wine, scraping up any bits on the bottom of the pan. Reduce mixture over high heat until about 1/3 cup remains. Add stock and adobo sauce; reduce until 3/4 cup of liquid is left. Strain mixture into a clean saucepan and heat to boiling; whisk in butter and season to taste with salt and pepper.

3. Place a large spoonful of sauce on each of two dinner plates and arrange pork medallions in the center of the sauce.

When Barbara Fenzl and Pamela Wischkaemper started Les Gourmettes in 1983, classes were so popular that they began inviting guest chefs from around the world. Although Wischkaemper moved to California in 1985, Fenzl has continued to run the school out of her Phoenix home and has written three Southwest cookbooks. For Southwest: The Beautiful Cookbook in 1994, she developed a sauce using chipotle chiles and raspberries that "goes beautifully with pork," she says. "Now that there are just two of us at home to cook for, I adapted the recipe to be quick, easy and delicious for empty-nesters. It's just as good for newlyweds or can be expanded for a dinner party."

POACHED PEARS

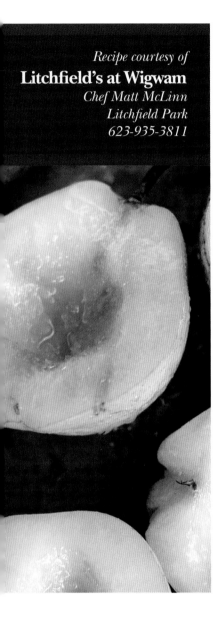

Recipe courtesy of
Litchfield's at Wigwam
Chef Matt McLinn
Litchfield Park
623-935-3811

SERVES 12

1 tablespoon	sugar
1/2 bottle	white wine (to cover)
6	D'anjou pears, peeled
1 tablespoon	fresh squeezed lemon juice
1 cup	water
1	sprig thyme
1	fresh bay leaf
1	star anise
1	cinnamon stick
1	salt
1	whole black pepper

1. Boil sugar and wine until sugar is completely dissolved. Add pears and bring to a boil. Reduce heat.

2. Add remaining ingredients and simmer uncovered until tender and easily poked with a fork, about 20 minutes. Allow to cool in liquid and serve.

The food speaks for itself at Litchfield's at the Wigwam Resort. Chef de Cuisine Brian Cooper owns the farm-to-table approach, working with local farmers to showcase the freshest seasonal ingredients, and making it a point to incorporate them into every dish. Most of his hot dishes are prepared in a wood-fired grill oven that fills the dining room with the smells of delicate burning wood chips.

GUACAMOLE TOSTADA

SERVES 6

6	avocados peeled and seeded
1/2 teaspoon	salt, to taste
1/2 teaspoon	garlic powder
1-2 ounces	Los Compadres hot sauce, or any hot sauce or salsa
	Fresh lime juice to taste
6	tostada shells
2-3 cups	shredded lettuce
2 cups	shredded Mexican blend cheese

1. Use potato masher to combine avocado, salt, garlic powder and hot sauce. Squeeze fresh lime into avocado mixture. Add more lime if desired.

2. Spread over tostada shells, top with shredded lettuce and cheese.

Recipe courtesy of
**Los Compadres
Mexican Restaurant**
*Chef Lucia Valdivia
Phoenix
602-265-1162*

The history of Los Compadres starts long before there ever was a "Los." In 1939, El Rey café in Miami, Arizona was started by our "Nana," Josephine Picaso. As her business grew, so did her family. Over the course of 20 years, she and her family established a total of thirteen restaurants in the state. Los Compadres was one of these establishments, later passed on to Josephine's daughter Lucia Valdivia. The tradition of family continues today with their children's menu options. Their Baby's Plate—shredded chicken or beef with beans and rice— or the Child's Plate—chico taco, rice and beans—are the perfect fix for children. For the older crowd, don't miss the Los Mexican Pizza, green chile strips, jalapeños, tomatoes, olives, green onion, guacamole and sour cream all atop a warm and crunchy flour tortilla.

HALIBUT VERACRUZANA

Recipe courtesy of
Los Olivos Mexican Patio
Chef Dora Valenzuela
Scottsdale
480-946-2256

Named for the olive trees planted along Second Street by Winfield Scott in 1896, Los Olivos is Scottsdale's oldest operating Mexican restaurant. It was founded by Alvaro and Elena Corral in 1946. Al's parents, Tomas and Cecilia, had come to Scottsdale in 1919, and originally used the old adobe building (expanded and remodeled over the years) as a bakery, pool hall and chapel. It was the hub of the Hispanic community for many years. The Corral family still owns and operates the restaurant (as well as a second location) today, dishing out comforting Sonoran-style food, including fabulous house-made flour tortillas.

SERVES 4

4	tomatoes, diced
2	bell peppers, diced
1	onion, diced
1	chile serrano, finely chopped
1/4 cup	green chile, diced
1/4 cup	tomato puree
2 tablespoons	olive oil
4	halibut fillets
1 tablespoon	salt
2 tablespoons	granulated garlic
1 tablespoons	black pepper
1-2 cups	water

1. In large saucepan, heat one tablespoon of oil. Add tomatoes, bell peppers and onion. Sauté for 4 minutes. Add tomato puree, serrano and green chile. Stir for two minutes. Add salt, pepper and garlic. Add one cup of water to vegetables. Add more if needed. You want the sauce to be a little thick, not runny, because as the vegetables cook they release liquid. Bring to a boil, cover, lower heat and simmer for 20 minutes. Keep warm until ready to serve.

2. Rinse and pat dry halibut. Salt and pepper filets on both sides. On a flat grill or large pan, heat one tablespoon of oil and cook filets until lightly browned on both sides.

3. Place cooked halibut on individual plates and top with enough sauce to cover.

SEAFOOD TACOS
WITH SPICY CABBAGE

Recipe courtesy of
Los Sombreros Café & Cantina
*Chef Azucena Tovar
Scottsdale
480-994-1799*

SERVES 6

1 pound	cod
5 ounces	shrimp
1 1/4 tablespoons	honey
1/2 cup	chopped onion
1 1/2 tablespoons	soy sauce
1/2 cup	adobo sauce
	Olive oil
18	small corn tortillas
	Garnishes: Spicy Cabbage, chopped tomato, chopped cilantro, thinly sliced radishes and avocado, guacamole, sour cream

1. Chop raw cod and shrimp. Stir together honey, onion, soy and adobo sauces, then mix the sauce into the chopped seafood.

2. Sauté the mixture in olive oil until the fish is cooked and the onions are translucent, about 10 minutes.

3. Spoon the mixture into warmed tortillas. Serve with garnishes on the side.

While many Arizona restaurants embrace the cuisine of Northern Mexico, Los Sombreros embodies a region that is often overlooked—Southern Mexico. For more than 15 years, Los Sombreros has been a beloved destination for regional cooking steeped in the traditions of Mexico. Using time-honored techniques and creative nuances, Chef-owner Azucena Tovar is known for her award-winning Mexican comfort food. It's easy to be captivated by the irresistible aromas wafting out of the central exhibition-style kitchen, as you dine on the rustically romantic patio.

SHREDDED BEEF CHIMICHANGA DE MACAYO

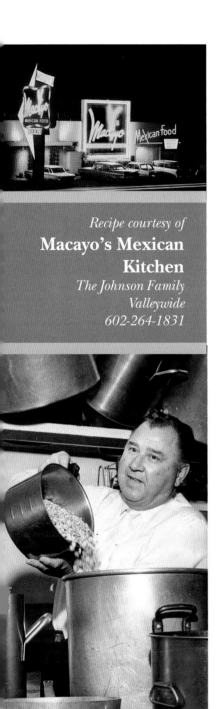

Recipe courtesy of
Macayo's Mexican Kitchen
The Johnson Family
Valleywide
602-264-1831

SERVES 6

SHREDDED BEEF RECIPE

2 pounds	boneless beef chuck
2 tablespoons	canola oil
1	large yellow onion, thinly sliced
2	garlic cloves, peeled and crushed
1 can, 4 ounces	green chilies, diced, drained, rinsed thoroughly
1 can, 8 ounces	tomatoes, diced in juice
	Water or beef broth to cover meat
1 teaspoon	garlic powder
	Salt to taste
	White ground pepper to taste

CHIMICHANGA DE MACAYO RECIPE (1 CHIMI)

1	flour tortilla, 13-inch
5 ounces	shredded beef, prepared
	Canola oil for frying
1/2 cup	relleno sauce
1/4 cup	sour cream
2 tablespoons	mixed cheese, shredded
1/2 tablespoon	diced tomatoes
	Canola oil

1. To prepare the shredded beef, in a large skillet or Dutch oven, sauté 2 tablespoons canola oil with garlic and onion until onions are translucent, about 4-6 minutes. Remove onions and garlic from skillet. Place meat in skillet and sauté over high heat, searing both sides. After meat has browned, add diced green chilies and diced tomatoes. Add water or beef broth to cover.

2. Reduce heat to medium low, cover pot and simmer for 2 hours, or until meat is tender. Remove meat to a cutting board and allow to cool. Shred meat using two large forks pulling in opposing directions. Transfer shredded meat into a bowl and add remaining sautéed garlic, onion, green chiles and diced tomatoes. Season meat and vegetable mixture with garlic powder, salt and white pepper.

3. To prepare a chimichanga, spread shredded beef across center of tortilla. Roll the tortilla burrito style, enclosing the filling and sealing the tortilla ends. Fill large fryer or deep pot halfway with canola oil. Heat to 355-365 degrees. When hot, place chimichanga into fryer. Use a flat spatula to hold the chimi and prevent opening during frying. Deep fry chimichanga to a golden brown, approximately 1-1 1/2 minutes, allow to drain.

4. To serve, cover with relleno sauce, top with sour cream, cheese and diced tomatoes.

When Woody and Victoria Johnson opened the first Macayo's in 1946, little did they know they started a Mexican restaurant epidemic that would spread Macayo's restaurants all over Arizona and Nevada. Today, the Johnson family owns 14 Arizona locations and four in Las Vegas. With a focus on community involvement and fresh, authentic Mexican cuisine, their traditions are served in every bite. Dine-in or take out with one of their party platters or catering options. Either way, there is no denying Macayo's traditional taste.

CRISPY PLA

Recipe courtesy of
Malee's on Main
Chef Deirdre Pain
Scottsdale
480-947-6042

For more than 24 years, Malee's on Main has been the heartbeat of Thai cuisine in Arizona. Zen-inspired design cues grace the space, transporting you to the land of a thousand smiles. Golden Buddhas, red upholstery and woven wood seats set the scene for a culinary journey through spice-laden, intensely flavorful authentic fare. Balance here is key, and Malee's has found the right mixture of spicy and sweet mouthwatering dishes with the perfect blend of traditional flavors, including lime, lemongrass, curry, pineapple and peppers.

SERVES 4

1	large fish fillet, about 8 to 10 ounces
2 cups	cornstarch
	Canola oil for frying

SAUCE

3/4 cup	sweet and sour sauce
1 teaspoon	crispy garlic
1 teaspoon	oyster sauce
1 teaspoon	fish sauce
1 teaspoon	lemon juice
1 teaspoon	paprika
1 teaspoon	cornstarch
	Cilantro for garnish

1. Cut fish fillet in half or keep whole. Dust with cornstarch. Fill large sauté pan with about 1-inch canola oil. Heat on medium heat, and when done, add fillet, in batches if necessary. Fry about 3-4 minutes, or until golden. Gently turn and cook an additional 3 minutes, or until crispy. Remove and keep warm while making sauce, or make sauce before frying fish.

2. In a medium size pan, combine sauce ingredients and cook over medium heat until sauce is thickens. Arrange cooked crispy fish on a platter and pour sauce over. Garnish with fresh cilantro.

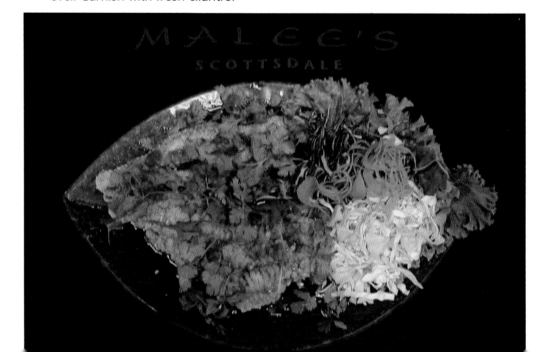

ALBONDIGAS SOUP

SERVES 10

STOCK

3 quarts	beef broth
1 cup	fresh roasted and diced green chilies or 2, 4 ounces cans
1 1/2 cups	celery, sliced
2	cloves garlic, minced
1 cup	carrots, sliced
1	large yellow onion, diced
1 10 ounce can	diced tomatoes with juice
	Salt and pepper to taste

MEATBALLS

1 1/4 pound	ground beef
2 1/2 tablespoons	raw rice
3 tablespoons	flour
1	egg
1 teaspoon	oregano (crush between your palms to release flavor)
1	clove garlic, minced
1	pinch cumin
	Salt and pepper to taste
	Sprigs of fresh cilantro

1. Put all stock ingredients in a large stockpot and cook over medium heat until vegetables are tender about 45 minutes. Meanwhile, prepare meatballs.

2. In mixing bowl, combine all meatballs ingredients, mixing well. Roll about a heaping teaspoon of meat into meatballs. Place on a tray in the refrigerator for about 30 minutes. Add to soup the last 20 minutes of cooking time. Garnish bowls of Albondigas with a sprig of fresh cilantro.

Recipe courtesy of
**Manuel's
Mexican Food**
*The Salazar Family
Valleywide*
602-957-7540

In 1964, Manuel and Alice Salazar followed in the footsteps of Manuel's sister Olivia Garcia (founder of Garcia's) to open their first Mexican restaurant on Indian School west of 32nd Street in Phoenix. It was such a hit that by the early '70s, the Salazars had opened a second location on Cave Creek Road (instantly mobbed with customers), expanding over the years to nine Valley-wide locations. Although two locations have closed in recent years, the remaining seven are still going strong. They're run by the Salazar's children and grandchildren, who get together every month to ensure that each Manuel's is as good as the original.

PUMPKIN SOUP

Recipe courtesy of
The Manzanita Restaurant
Chef Randy Hale
Cornville
928-634-8851

It's not every day you come across a German-inspired menu, unless, that is, you are dining at The Manzanita Restaurant in Cornville. Founded more than 20 years ago by Swiss-trained master-Chef Albert Kramer III, the place offers classic German dishes like Wiener schnitzel, beef roulade and schweinshaxe with a slight continental twist, serving them with traditional sides of German potato salad, sauerkraut or red cabbage. But The Manzanita does not stop there; it also serves American and European specialties like filet mignon served with sautéed mushrooms, and grilled Frenched lamb chops served with mint jelly and a demi-glace.

SERVES 20 (8 OUNCE PORTIONS)

6 cups	pumpkin puree, fresh or canned
1/2 gallon	chicken broth
1 pint	heavy cream
1 cup	orange juice
1 pound	brown sugar
1/2 tablespoon	ground white pepper
1/2 tablespoon	pumpkin pie spice
1/2 tablespoon	ground nutmeg
1/2 tablespoon	ground cinnamon
1/4 cup	butter
1/2	yellow onion, diced small
2 tablespoons	dry sherry (optional)

1. To make fresh puree, cut pumpkin into large pieces and place into a deep baking dish. Pour enough orange juice over the pieces to keep them moist and prevent scorching. Sprinkle a little brown sugar, pumpkin pie spice and cinnamon (not the measurements given above) over the pieces and bake at 350 degrees until tender, about 2 hours. Scrape pumpkin from ski. Pour juice from the pan and pumpkin flesh into a blender and puree.

2. Sauté onion in butter until golden caramel in color.

3. Heat chicken broth, Add puree and other spices, bring to light boil. Reduce heat and simmer for 10 minutes stirring frequently.

4. Adjust seasoning as needed. Pumpkins, including commercially prepared puree, have different tastes and richness of flavor, so adjust accordingly

5. Add sherry and stir to blend. Serve.

LOBSTER MASHED POTATOES

Recipe courtesy of
Mastro's Restaurants
Chef Brian Kohl
Valleywide
818-598-5656

Take one step into Mastro's and you'll walk into a forgotten era of classic opulence. Mastro's is the ideal place to stimulate the senses. Take in the sounds of a sizzling New York steak served on a 400-degree plate. Savor the juicy, hand-cut USDA prime steaks, fresh seafood, larger-than-life sides and signature warm butter cake. The cosmopolitan atmosphere is reminiscent of Manhattan and offers an intimate dining experience. The original Mastro's Steakhouse opened in North Scottsdale, with a legacy that continues to thrive.

SERVES 6

5 pounds	peeled raw potatoes, cut 3"x3"
1 1/2 cups	heavy cream
1/2 pound	salted butter, diced in 1" cubes
3/4 tablespoon	iodized salt
1/2 teaspoon	ground white pepper
1/2 cup	roasted garlic
3 pounds	live Maine lobster, steamed, chilled, shelled, and tail cut into 8 pieces leaving the claws intact.
6 ounces	salted butter
1 1/2 teaspoon	Old Bay seasoning
1 1/2 tablespoon	charred scallions, 1/4" cut

1. Roast two whole bulbs of elephant garlic in a 350-degree oven till tender. Discard skins and puree.

2. Peel and boil potatoes till they are tender. Strain and place in a Kitchen Aid mixer.

3. Bring cream and butter to a boil in a saucepan. Then, mix potatoes with the whisk attachment on low speed while adding cream mixture. Add garlic and seasoning. Turn the speed up to medium high and whisk until smooth and creamy.

4. Melt the butter with the lobster, Old Bay and scallions.

5. Gently lay the mashed potatoes in a serving bowl, maintaining as much height as possible. Pour the lobster butter mixture over the mashed potatoes. Present the claws on top.

CHORIZO PORCHETTA
WITH GARLIC CREMA AND WHITE BEAN PUREE

Recipe courtesy of
The Mission
Chef Matt Carter
Scottsdale
480-636-5005

The Mission emanates Old World elegance combined with Latin accents and contemporary design. Upon entering, guests are embraced by a Himalayan salt block wall, rustic chandeliers and flickering candlelight. Chef Matt Carter draws culinary influence from Spain, Mexico, Central and South America and utilizes French techniques to enrich every dish with culture, using pecan and mesquite wood. The menu includes such fare as Crispy Cola Pork, Duck Carnitas Enchiladas and Roasted Organic Butternut Squash.

SERVES 6-8

CHORIZO

1 pound	ground pork
4	dried New Mexican chilies
2 tablespoons	Spanish paprika
1 tablespoon	cumin
1/2 cup	apple cider vinegar
4 cloves	roasted garlic
	Salt and pepper to taste

1. Roast chilies for 2 minutes in a 400 degree oven
2. Puree in food processor to make a powder
3. Combine all ingredients and reserve

PORCHETTA

1 6-pound	pork shoulder
1 pound	homemade chorizo
	Salt and pepper to taste
	pork lard
	butcher's twine

1. Butterfly the shoulder so it lays flat like an open book
2. Season the inside and add chorizo to either of the small sides
3. Roll your shoulder around the chorizo and continue until it meets the other side and the chorizo is encased inside
4. Truss your shoulder with butcher's twine so it's nice and secure and season heavily with salt and pepper
5. Roast in a deep hotel pan in a 250-degree oven until the internal temperature registers 150 degrees F
6. Remover from oven and add enough pork lard to cover
7. Cover with aluminum foil and continue cooking for 4 more hours
8. Allow to cool in pan until fat has solidified
9. Remove the porchetta and remove the twine, slice into six 10 ounce portions
10. Reheat on a grill and serve with white bean puree and garlic crema

WHITE BEAN PUREE

1/2 cup	white beans (soaked overnight)
1	carrot
1	celery stalk
1/2	white onion
	chicken stock
1 cup	milk
6	roasted cherry tomatoes
1	lime (juiced)
	handful of arugula
	Salt and pepper to taste

1. In a large pot combine beans, vegetables, and cover with chicken stock
2. Bring to a boil and then reduce to a simmer for 45 minutes to and 1 hour
3. Strain and remove vegetables and puree with milk, tomatoes, and lime juice
4. Fold in your arugula, season and reserve (Serve Hot)

GARLIC CREMA

1 large clove	elephant garlic (roasted)
1/4 cup	sweetened condensed milk
1/4 cup	heavy cream
	Salt and pepper to taste
	handful of arugula

1. Puree all ingredients together
2. Reserve and serve hot

SHERRY GASTRIQUE

1	bottle of dry sherry wine
1	bottle of sherry vinegar
2 cups	sugar
2	Morita chilies

1. In a heavy saucepot add your wine and reduce by half
2. Add your bottle of sherry vinegar and bring to a boil
3. Add in your sugar and stir until all has dissolved
4. Reduce to a simmer and add chilies
5. Reduce your liquid until it becomes glazy (about 1 hour)
6. Remove chilies and drizzle atop porchetta for the finishing touch

MOLLY'S SPECIAL STEAK AND GRAVY

Recipe courtesy of
Molly Butler Lodge
Chef Ruben Irigoyan
Greer
928-735-7226

Long before Arizona became a state, Molly Butler Lodge gave shelter to hunters, fishermen and visitors traveling to or through Greer. In return, passersby would share daily chores, helping to maintain the frontier lodge. Finally, Molly's daughter worked up the courage to start charging guests 25 cents per meal. Today Molly Butler's old lodge is still well-known for its extreme hospitality as well as whipping up a meal that "is better than your grandma's."

SERVES 5

STEAK

2 pounds	lean sirloin steak roast, cut into 1/2-inch medallions
1 tablespoon	Montreal steak seasoning

MASHED POTATOES

3 pounds	Yukon potatoes
1/2 pound	butter
1/2 tablespoon	pepper
1 tablespoon	salt
1/2 tablespoon	dried parsley
1 cup	heavy cream

GRAVY

1/3 pound	butter
1 cup	flour
4 ounces	ground beef
1 tablespoon	pepper
1 tablespoon	ham base
1 tablespoon	salt
1 can, 12 ounces	evaporated milk
6 cups	water

1. Heat grill to medium high heat. When hot, lightly oil the grates and add steak. Grill 4-5 minutes a side. Remove and sprinkle the Montreal steak seasoning. Allow to cool slightly and cut into cut into 1/2-inch medallions.

2. Bring a pot of salted water to a boil. Add unpeeled potatoes, and simmer on medium high heat, for 45 minutes to 1 hour, or until soft. Drain water. Add the butter, pepper, salt, parsley and heavy cream to potatoes in the pot. Use a wire whisk to mix the ingredients and to mash the potatoes.

3. To prepare the gravy, melt the butter in a saucepan over medium heat. Add the ground beef and cook until golden brown, stirring occasionally. Add pepper, ham base and salt. Reduce heat to low, and continue cooking ground beef for 5 minutes. Add the evaporated milk and water. Heat the gravy until it begins to boil, and then remove from the stove top.

4. Place steak and mashed potatoes on plates, and cover with hot gravy.

WHOLE ROAST PRIME RIB

Recipe courtesy of
Monti's La Casa Vieja
Chef Alberto Hernandez
Tempe
480-967-7594

SERVES UP TO 20

1 14-16 pound, 7 bone	whole prime rib roast
1/2 cup	garlic powder
1/2 cup	Kosher salt
4 tablespoons	ground black pepper
1/2 cup	dry rosemary
1/2 cup	Cajun seasoning
10 – 15	bay leaves
1/4 cup	1/4 cup Spanish paprika

1. Start by removing the fat cap from the prime rib. Apply seasonings evenly to both sides of the meat. Let sit for about 1 hour. Preheat oven to 250 degrees.

2. Roast in oven at 250 degrees for about 4 hours for rare to 6 hours for medium well. Remove. Allow to rest about 10 minutes before cutting and serving.

When dining at Monti's La Casa Vieja, visitors step into Tempe's original pioneer home and the oldest continuously occupied building in the area, dating all the way back to 1871. Monti's strives to keep the original aspect of the structure intact, and serves popular entrees such as Herb Crusted Prime Rib, which is slowly roasted to seal in flavor, juiciness and tenderness, or the Full Monti Burger, loaded with BBQ sauce, bacon, cheddar, pepper jack cheese and crispy onion rings.

SOUTHERN FRIED CHICKEN

SERVES 5

5 pounds	chicken, cut into pieces
3	eggs
1/2 cup	red pepper
2 cups	all-purpose flour
	Seasoning salt to taste
	Black pepper to taste
	Paprika seasoning mix
	Oil for frying

1. Wash chicken in cold water. Pat dry. In a medium size bowl, beat eggs. Add red pepper to eggs and stir until blended. In another bowl, combine flour, seasoning salt and black pepper.

2. Season chicken with paprika mix. Dip the seasoned chicken in the egg, and then coat well in the flour mixture.

3. Heat the oil to 350 degrees in a deep pot. Do not fill the pot more than 1/2 full with oil. Add chicken in batches, and fry for about 5-8 minutes, or until no pink is left in the meat.

Recipe courtesy of
Mrs. White's Golden Rule Café
Chef Elizabeth J. White
Phoenix
602-262-9256

The only rule at this down-home spot is to come hungry and leave happy. Mrs. White's was established in 1964 and for over 50 years has been dishing out mouthwatering, golden brown Southern-style fried chicken. If soul food is what you are searching for, the golden yellow brick building on Jefferson Street is the place to eat. The food has soul because the family cooking it has heart.

Photo: Michael McNamara

CURED SALMON
WITH BASIL OIL AND SOY-GLAZED ALMONDS

SERVES 4

Recipe courtesy of
**Nobuo
at Teeter House**
*Chef Nobuo Fukuda
Phoenix
602-254-0600*

The historic Teeter House, a graceful, circa-1899 red brick pyramid cottage in Downtown Phoenix's Heritage Square, may be an unexpected place to find a Japanese restaurant, but considering Chef Nobuo Fukuda's inventive take on Japan's traditional cuisine, it's a surprisingly beautiful fit. After working in many Scottsdale restaurants— including the legendary Sea Saw, where he won a James Beard Award for his distinctive tasting menus— Fukuda opened this charming izakaya in 2010, where he serves tapas-style dishes that merge his Japanese sensibility with Arizona-grown ingredients. A longtime favorite at his restaurants, Fukuda's cured-salmon recipe goes especially well with a dry or sparkling Rosé.

1 pound	sushi grade sockeye salmon fillet, pin bones removed
1/2 cup	sea or Kosher salt
1/4 cup	packed brown sugar
1/4 cup	roughly chopped fresh mint
1/4 cup	roughly chopped fresh basil
2 tablespoons	grated lemon zest
2 tablespoons	grated lime zest
2 cups	white wine, preferably Sauvignon Blanc
2 tablespoons	shaved Pecorino-Romano cheese
1 tablespoon	basil oil
1 tablespoon	balsamic soy reduction

BASIL OIL

	Pinch of salt
1 bunch	basil leaves, stemmed (about 1/4 pound)
1/4 cup	grape seed oil

BALSAMIC-SOY REDUCTION

1 cup	balsamic vinegar
2 tablespoons	soy sauce

SOY-GLAZED ALMONDS

1/2 cup	whole almonds
1 teaspoon	soy sauce
1 teaspoon	sake
1 teaspoon	mirin
	Mixed fresh Asian greens, optional, dressed lightly with olive oil and citrus juice if desired

1. To prepare salmon, lay plastic wrap in a 9-by-12-inch baking dish and cover with a layer of salt. Lay salmon, skin-side down, on the layer of salt. Cover the salmon with the rest of the salt. On top of salt, evenly spread a layer of brown sugar, mint, basil and citrus zests. Wrap plastic wrap tightly around the entire salmon 3 or 4 times, being careful not to leave any openings. Refrigerate for 48 hours. Remove, unwrap, and wash under ice cold water. Dry with paper towels. Place the fish back in the cleaned baking dish, add the wine, and let soak for 30 minutes. Remove and refrigerate until ready to use.

2. For basil oil, bring a pot of water to a boil and add a pinch of salt. Plunge the basil leaves into the boiling water. Remove and strain. Quickly place the leaves in an ice bath. When cool, squeeze out extra water and place in blender with grape seed oil. Blend well. Strain the mixture through a cheesecloth-lined strainer, reserving the oil and discarding the solids. Use for salmon, and store remainder in the refrigerator for up to 2 weeks.

3. For balsamic-soy reduction, bring the vinegar and soy sauce to a boil. Reduce the heat immediately and simmer the mixture until reduced to a syrupy consistency, about 10 minutes.

4. For almonds, heat oven to 300 degrees. Spread the almonds in a pie pan and toast in the oven for about 20 minutes, shaking the pan occasionally. In a frying pan over medium heat, cook the toasted almonds with the soy sauce, sake and mirin until the nuts absorb the liquid. Remove quickly so that the almonds do not burn; set aside to dry.

5. To serve, remove salmon, unwrap, and wash under ice cold water. Dry with paper towels. Place the fish back in the cleaned baking dish, add wine and soak for 30 minutes. Remove. With a long, thin, very sharp knife, slice the salmon into 1/4 inch slices and fan out slices on 4 plates. Drizzle each with 1 tablespoon basil oil and 1 tablespoon balsamic-soy reduction. Sprinkle with soy-glazed almonds and Pecorino Romano cheese. Serve with Asian greens if desired.

Photo credit: Geoff Reed

SHRIMP & GRITS WITH HAM-HOCK GUMBO

Recipe courtesy of
NOCA
Chef Matt Taylor
Phoenix
602-956-6622

Situated among the hustle bustle of 32nd Street, just north of Camelback Road is where you can find NOCA owner Eliot Wexler and Executive Chef Matt Taylor serving inimitable sandwiches for lunch and entrees for dinner. Seasonal items are kept in mind, and of course, the chef's current mood is always taken into account when preparing the menu. On a lunch break, treat your belly to sandwiches filled with house-made bacon, house-roasted turkey or anchiote-braised Berkshire pork. For a taste of the dinner menu, try one of NOCA's handmade pastas or artisan grains. If preparing Sunday dinner isn't your forte, come in for Sunday Simple Supper, a changing fresh and delicious three-course supper.

SERVES 4

2 cups	flour
1 1/2 cups	vegetable oil
4 cups	whole milk
1 cup	white grits (recommend Anson Mills Coarse White Grits available at ansonmills.com)
4 tablespoons	butter
4 tablespoons	mascarpone cheese
	Salt to taste
1	white onion
2	green jalapeños
4	celery stalks
2	green bell pepper
3	white shrimp with shells, cleaned
1	ham hock split (recommend bentonscountryhams2.com)
1 pound	Andouille sausage, diced (recommend Jacobs Andouille available at cajunsausage.com)
6 tablespoons	Cajun seasoning blend
1 tablespoon	filé powder (available at cajunsausage.com or most grocery stores)

1. To make roux, heat vegetable oil on low heat in a large skillet, and slowly incorporate flour. Stir constantly until mixture is very dark brown, or darker than peanut butter, and smells sweet and nutty. This step takes a few hours. If roux burns, start over.

2. In a separate pot, bring the milk to a simmer over medium heat. Add the grits, stirring occasionally until the granules are soft. Set aside until ready to serve. Finish grits with butter, mascarpone, and salt to taste just before serving.

3. Dice vegetables to about the size of your small finger nail. Save trimmings for stock.

4. In a large pot combine trimmings, shrimp shells from the shrimp after they have been cleaned, and the ham hock. Cover completely with water and simmer over medium heat while preparing remainder of the dish.

5. In a large pot combine diced Andouille and roux. Slowly cook until sausage is tender, and some of its natural juices have been released.

6. Add diced onions, jalapeños, celery, bell peppers, and garlic to pot with Andouille and roux. Continue to slowly cook until vegetables are tender. Add Cajun seasoning.

7. Strain stock reserving ham hock. Carefully add liquid to pot of Andouille and roux and pick all meat and skin from the ham-hock bones. Dice meat and skin, and then add to pot as well.

8. In saucepan melt 3 tablespoons of butter. Add shrimp, and cook lightly, about 3-4 minutes, to prevent them from turning rubbery. In four bowls divide up finished grits, and shrimp. Spoon over equal portions of gumbo.

9. Garnish with fried parsley leaves, sliced scallions or a nice slice of smoky/salty country ham.

SPINACH CON QUESO

Recipe courtesy of
The Original Garcia's Las Avenidas
Olivia Garcia, Owner
Phoenix
602-272-5584

Encouraged by the compliments she received on her cooking, Olivia Garcia talked her husband, Julio, into opening a small take-out counter in West Phoenix in 1956. When they could no longer accommodate the crowds, the couple moved to larger quarters in the same neighborhood in 1959, opening an upscale version of the original (called Garcia's del Este) in Scottsdale to instant success in 1970. With the help of their children, the family expanded to three Valley locations, eventually partnering with financial backers to create a national franchise chain called Garcia's of Scottsdale. The Garcias sold their interest in Garcia's of Scottsdale in the mid-'80s, keeping The Original Garcia's Las Avenidas in the West Valley neighborhood where their success story began.

135

SERVES 6

2 pounds	jalapeño pepper cheese loaf
2 cups	whole milk, divided
1 1/4 cup	chopped frozen spinach , thawed and squeezed dry
3/4 cup	fresh tomatoes, diced
3/4 cup	bell peppers, diced
1/2 cup	white onion, diced

1. Grate cheese loaf and place in double boiler. Add 8 ounces milk. Simmer over medium heat until cheese is melted.

2. When cheese has melted, stir in spinach, tomatoes, peppers and onion. Add more milk until desired thickness is reached. Serve with chips.

GRILLED LAMB LOIN CHOPS
WITH WILD MUSHROOM POLENTA CAKES,
NOGALES SPAGHETTI SQUASH, NOPALITO MINT JELLY

SERVES 4

2 tablespoons	olive oil, divided
1/2 pound	shiitake mushrooms, chopped
1	medium spaghetti squash
2 cups	heavy cream
1 cup	whole milk
1 cup	yellow corn meal
12	3-4 ounce lamb loin chops
1	4 ounce can nopalitos
1	small jalapeño, seeded
3/4 cup	mint jelly
1/4 cup	cream cheese
	Salt and pepper to taste
2-3	eggs, beaten

Recipe courtesy of
The Peacock Room at Hassayampa Inn
Chef Jason Perkins
Prescott
928-778-9434

1. Heat sauté pan on medium heat. Add oil, and when hot, add shiitakes. Season with salt and pepper. Sauté until tender, about 5-7 minutes. Set aside. Cut spaghetti squash lengthwise and remove seeds. Bring large steamer pot to a boil and place squash in steamer basket. Steam for 12 minutes and cool in ice water immediately to stop cooking. Use a fork to scrape string-like flesh from the squash. Heat large skillet on medium high heat. Add 1 tablespoon olive oil, and sauté for about 4 minutes. Season with salt and pepper. Set aside.

2. In a separate pot, bring cream and milk to a hard boil, rapidly whisk in corn meal until completely incorporated. Cook 5 minutes, stirring constantly. Reduce heat to low, and stir in mushrooms and cream cheese. Season to taste. Take cooked polenta and pour into a 5-by-9 inch baking pan. Cool 1 to 2 hours before cutting into 2-by-1-inch squares.

3. Drain nopalitos and puree in food processor with one small seeded jalapeño. In a separate bowl, blend mixture with jelly until smooth. Cover and chill in the refrigerator.

4. Heat outdoor grill on high heat. Season lamb with salt and pepper. When grill is hot, lightly oil grates and place lamb on grill. Grill for about 4-5 minutes a side. Place cut polenta into egg batter. Heat non-stick skillet on high. Lightly spray with cooking oil and grill polenta cakes, in batches, for about 2 minutes a side, or until golden brown.

5. Set 3 polenta cakes in a row and top with lamb loin. Place squash and drizzle jelly mixture over lamb and serve.

For more than 80 years, The Hassayampa Inn has been checking in famous guests and true Arizona characters, from miners and cowboys, to actors and dignitaries, and all those vibrant people needed good food to go along with their stay at the inn. Today, guests dine at The Peacock Dining Room in an elegant setting. Long and short framed mirrors hang on the walls, fall-inspired leaf prints decorate the warm, round booths and classic, lily of the valley-inspired lampshades surround the picturesque Peacock Room.

ENCHILADAS SUIZAS

SERVES 4

SAUCE

3 cups	water
10	tomatillos, husk removed
2	jalapeños
1/3	white onion, sliced
1/3 cup	cilantro
1	clove garlic
1 teaspoon	salt
1/2 teaspoon	pepper

ENCHILADAS

12-15	small corn tortillas
4 cups	shredded rotisserie chicken (available at grocery stores)
2-3 cups	grated Monterey Jack cheese
1 cup	sour cream
1 cup	grated Asadero cheese

1. Lightly boil tomatillos in 3 cups water for 20 minutes. Drain and add tomatillos, with remaining ingredients, to blender. Blend until smooth and set aside.

2. Gently warm tortillas on griddle or stove, then dip in vegetable oil. Place 1/3 cup chicken and 1/4 cup Jack cheese at edge of each tortilla and roll them up.

3. Preheat oven to 350 degrees. Place seam side down in lightly greased 10-by 15-inch baking dish. Pour tomatillo sauce over enchiladas, dot enchiladas with sour cream and bake for 30 minutes. Before serving, sprinkle with grated Asadero cheese.

Recipe courtesy of
Pepe's Taco Villa
Lucy and Jose Acosta, Owners
Phoenix
602-242-0379

Monterrey-born Pepe Acosta was a famous Hispanic radio announcer on KPHX for 40 years. His wife, Dora, who often cooked for Pepe's employer Ray Korte of Ray Korte Chevrolet, was equally famous for her Mexican food. In 1981, the couple decided to capitalize on their good name. They opened Pepe's, serving chilaquiles, mole and other authentic specialties long before such dishes were mainstream in Phoenix. The Acostas' children—Lucy and Jose—now run the business and although the menu has expanded over the years, many customers still come for the signature Taco Siberia and Taco Monterrey.

LOBSTER BISQUE

Recipe courtesy of
Petite Maison
Chef James Porter
Scottsdale
480-941-6887

The size of the restaurant is in fact petite, but the food is anything but. Hidden away amid the night club scene in the heart of Old Town Scottsdale stands Petite Maison. Once you step inside this cozy French bistro, it feels more like the South of France than south of Camelback. Glowing chandeliers hanging from the ceiling dimly light the dining room, which is surrounded by wood-paneled walls. The culinary expertise of Executive Chef James Porter allows diners to experience the tastes of France Tuesdays through Sundays.

SERVES 4

3-pound	live lobster
1	medium onion
1	celery rib
1	carrot
1	vine-ripened tomato
1	head garlic
2 tablespoons	olive oil
2 tablespoons	chopped fresh tarragon leaves
2 tablespoons	chopped fresh thyme leaves
1	bay leaf
8	black peppercorns
1/2 cup	brandy
1/2 cup	dry Sherry
4 cups	fish stock
1/2 cup	heavy cream
1 1/2 tablespoons	cornstarch
2 tablespoons	water
	Salt and pepper to taste

1. Fill a 6-quart kettle three fourths full with salted water and bring to a boil. Plunge lobster headfirst into water and cook, covered, over high heat 8 minutes.

2. Transfer lobster with tongs to a large bowl and in a measuring cup reserve 2 cups cooking liquid. Let lobster stand until cool enough to handle. Working over a bowl to catch the juices, twist off tail and claws and reserve juices. Reserve tomalley and discard head sacs and any roe. Remove meat from claws and tail, reserving shells and lobster body. (Lobster meat will not be cooked through.) Coarsely chop meat and transfer to a bowl. Chill lobster meat, covered.

3. Chop onion, celery, carrot, and tomato and halve garlic head crosswise. In a 6-quart heavy kettle heat oil over moderately high heat until hot but not smoking and sauté reserved lobster shells and body, stirring occasionally, 8 minutes. Add vegetables, garlic, herbs, peppercorns, brandy, and Sherry and simmer, stirring, until almost all liquid is evaporated, about 5 minutes. Add stock and reserved tomalley and cooking liquid. Simmer mixture, uncovered, stirring occasionally, 1 hour.

4. Pour mixture through a fine sieve into a large saucepan, pressing on and discarding solids. Add cream and simmer bisque 5 minutes. In a small bowl stir together cornstarch and water and whisk into bisque. Simmer bisque, stirring, 2 minutes to allow to thicken slightly. Add lobster meat with any reserved juices and simmer bisque 1 minute, or until lobster meat is just cooked through. Season bisque with salt and pepper.

BEEF TARTARE

Recipe courtesy of
Pink Pony
Reed Groban, Owner
Scottsdale
480-945-6697

Since 1949, Pink Pony has been a Scottsdale landmark for great steaks and a serious baseball memorabilia collection. Since the original owners, the Brileys, sold the place in 2009, Pink Pony has passed through several hands until finally reaching home base. Today Reed Groban, former executive chef at the Fairmont Scottsdale Princess, has modernized the menu, while preserving the restaurant's beloved baseball history. Take a swing at their filet mignon with a loaded baked potato, or Braised Short-rib Crepes with Garlic Flan and Bone Marrow. For the sweet tooth, try the pear-cranberry pie with pumpkin pie ice cream.

SERVES 1

3 1/2 ounces	tenderloin, chopped into small pieces
3 teaspoons	chopped white anchovies
2 1/4 teaspoons	capers, minced
2 1/4 teaspoons	Dijon
2 1/4 teaspoon	Worcestershire
2 1/4	orange zest
3 teaspoons	lemon juice
	Sea salt, to taste
	Pepper, to taste
4	Kettle cooked potato chips
1	egg yolk, lightly poached
2 1/4	olive oil
2 1/4	chopped parsley
2 1/4	chiffonade chives micro greens
	Fleur de Sel for seasoning
2 tablespoons	beer mustard

1. In mixing bowl, add tenderloin with anchovies, capers, Dijon, Worcestershire, zest, lemon juice, sea salt and pepper.

2. Pour in medium ring mold on plate. Garnish with chips, parsley, micros and egg yolk. Season with Fleur de Sel. Place miso spoon with beer mustard on plate.

PINNACLE PEAK PATIO COWBOY BEANS

Recipe courtesy of
Pinnacle Peak Patio
Chef "Big" Marv Dickson
Scottsdale
480-585-1599

SERVES 15-20

2 1/2 pounds	dried pinto beans
1	small ham hock or 1/2 cup chopped ham
1	large yellow onion, diced
2 tablespoons	salt
2 tablespoons	oregano
1 tablespoon	black pepper
3 ounces	chopped green chiles

1. Wash beans and remove any debris. Add all ingredients to pot and cover with 1 inch of water. Bring to a low boil and cover. Simmer until tender, about 3 hours. Keep adding water to just cover beans. For the best beans, cover and refrigerate overnight. Reheat the next day and serve.

Take one glance at the ties dangling from the ceiling and the business cards stapled to the walls, and you'll know you're dining at Pinnacle Peak Patio. Since 1961, "Big" Marv Dickson has been firing up the grills and serving all-time favorites like finger-lickin' baby back ribs and mesquite-grilled steaks. When you dine at Pinnacle Peak Patio, you'd better be hungry and you better come casual because this old cowboy hideaway strictly enforces its "no necktie policy" as part of its down-home hospitality.

CRAB CAKES WITH CREOLE MUSTARD

SERVES 6 ENTREES OR 12 APPETIZERS

Recipe courtesy of
Piñon Bistro
Chef Donna Fulton
Cottonwood
928-649-0234

closed mid-June
to mid-September

CRABCAKES

1 pound	fresh Dungeness crab
1/2	green bell pepper
1	celery stalk
1	small onion
2 tablespoons	Dijon mustard
3	whole eggs
4 cups	fresh bread crumbs from good quality bread
1/2 pound	unsalted butter for clarifying and sautéing

SAUCE

2 cups	heavy cream
1 cup	sour cream
2 tablespoons	Creole mustard
2 shakes	Worcestershire
1/4 teaspoon	salt
1/4 teaspoon	white and black pepper
	Pinch of cayenne pepper

1. Finely chop then combine bell pepper, celery and onion. Add the Dijon mustard, eggs and mix well. Add bread crumbs and mix until soaked. Add the crab and toss until evenly distributed throughout. Form crab cakes by cupping with hand. 1 – 1.5 inches for appetizer and 2-3 inches for entrees.

2. In clarified butter, sauté over medium-low heat until golden brown and cooked throughout.

*To clarify butter:

   - Cut butter in chunks.

   - Place small saucepan over low heat.

   - once melted skim off any white floating on top.

   - Pour off the butter into a separate container, being careful to avoid the white milk solids on the bottom of the pan.

3. To make sauce, in saucepan combine sour and heavy cream, Creole mustard, Worcestershire sauce, salt, white and black pepper, cayenne pepper over low heat. Stir until well blended and simmer for about 15 minutes, stirring occasionally.

Chef-owners Terri Clements and Donna Fulton dropped out of the corporate world, and after a year and a half of travel, settled in Cottonwood, the heart of Northern Arizona's wine country. At their intimate bistro, decorated with a changing display of local art, they channel their grandmothers, making everything from scratch, showcasing Arizona wines and incorporating local figs and pomegranates into their seasonal menu. The bistro's crunchy-edged crab cakes are a customer favorite. Serve them with crusty bread to mop up every creamy drop of Creole mustard sauce.

ROASTED EGGPLANT PARMIGIANA

SERVES 6-8

5 pounds	Japanese eggplant
1	large yellow onion
2 pounds	ripe tomatoes, preferably heirloom
4	fresh basil leaves
2 cloves	garlic, smashed
about 1/4 cup	extra virgin olive oil
1/4 pound	grated Parmigianno - Reggiano

1. Preheat oven to 450 degrees. Peel eggplant and roughly chop into approximately 3-inch pieces. Roughly chop onion into similar sized pieces. Quarter tomatoes and season with salt, pepper, garlic and basil.

2. In a large baking pan or sheet pan, add eggplant and onion and coat liberally with olive oil. Spread evenly in pan so not crowded, and bake about 15 minutes, or until eggplant begins to brown. Remove from oven and loosen from pan.

3. Add tomatoes and spread ingredients evenly in pan. Return to oven for 15 minutes. Remove from oven and transfer contents to 13-inch x 9-inch baking dish. The tomato mixture should fit snuggly. Cover with grated Parmigiano and return to oven for about 10 minutes, or until cheese is golden brown. Let rest 15 minutes, and serve warm or at room temperature.

Founded in 1988 and originally located in the back of a grocery store at Camelback and Central, James Beard Award-winning Chef Chris Bianco's celebrated pizzeria has been a part of Heritage Square, its current location, since 1996, occupying the circa-1929 Baird Machine Shop building. Unlike most of its neighbors, the handsome red brick structure sits on its original plot and was added to the National Register of Historic Places in 1985. Along with the wood-fired pizzas that have made it a destination, the restaurant celebrates local farm products, as illustrated by Bianco's interpretation of this classic (and normally fried) eggplant dish. He substitutes typical Black Beauty eggplant (which may need to be salted and drained of bitterness and moisture), for local violetta, a slender and sweet Japanese eggplant that doesn't need to be salted, and thus retains its natural sweet flavor and balanced moisture. Roasting instead of frying not only leads to a healthier version, but also adds a deeper savory-sweet flavor profile.

Recipe courtesy of
Pizzeria Bianco
Chef Chris Bianco
Phoenix
602-258-8300

CHICKEN TERRINE

SERVES 3-4

3 tablespoons	olive oil
3	shallots, diced
3	garlic cloves, peeled and diced
1	chicken, bones removed and cut into pieces
5	eggs
1 1/4 cups	heavy cream
	Nutmeg
	Salt/pepper

1. Preheat oven to 350 degrees. Heat a sauté pan on medium heat. Add olive oil, and when hot, add shallots and garlic. Sauté about 5 minutes. Remove from pan and cool.

2. Place chicken and eggs in a food processor. Pulse until completely blended. Add cream and seasoning. Pulse again until blended. Add shallot-garlic mixture and pulse until blended. Place mixture in a greased pâté mold. Cook in oven for 1 hour or until chicken is completely cooked.

Recipe courtesy of
Posh Restaurant
Chef Josh Hebert
Scottsdale
480-663-7674

Dine at Posh and you won't find a menu… anywhere. Not because they don't serve food (they do, and oh-so-well), but because Chef Joshua Hebert has built an improvisational restaurant that offers from four to 12 courses based on what you do and don't like. Simply cross off ingredients from the nightly list and let the show begin with dishes such as Kobe Beef with Pickled Ramps and Wasabi Butter, or Seared Monkfish with Crushed Peas, Roasted Peppers and Pommes Anna.

BRAISED ARIZONA BEEF
WITH WINTER SQUASH AND APPLE GREMOLATA

SERVES 6

5 pounds	chuck roast
1 cup	vegetable oil
3	large onions, cut into large pieces
3	carrots, peeled and cut into 1/2 inch pieces
6	ribs celery, cut into 1/2 inch pieces
2 cups	red wine
1/2	head of garlic
2	fresh bay leaves
4 sprigs	of fresh thyme
2 sprigs	of fresh rosemary
1/4 cup	red wine vinegar
4 cups	beef stock
	Salt and pepper

FOR THE SQUASH "MASH"

2	large butternut squash
2	large acorn squash
1/2 cup	vegetable oil
1 tablespoon	white wine vinegar
	Salt and pepper
1 cup	butter

FOR THE APPLE GREMOLATA

2	Granny Smith apples, peeled and diced
1/4 cup	chopped parsley
	Zest of 1 lemon
1/4 cup	olive oil
	Salt and pepper

1. Preheat oven to 350 degrees. Season beef well with salt and pepper, and allow to rest for 10-15 minutes. In a large roasting pan, add vegetable oil and heat to medium high. Add beef in batches and sear on all sides. Remove and set aside. Add carrots, celery and onions and sauté until lightly browned, about 5-7 minutes. Remove vegetables and pour out any excess oil. Add red wine and deglaze the pan. Reduce heat to medium low and simmer until wine is reduced in half. Add garlic, fresh herbs, red wine vinegar and beef stock. Return beef and vegetables to the pan. Cover and roast for 3-4 hours, stirring every hour until the beef is tender.

2. For squash, cut butternut and acorn in half. Remove seeds and lightly coat with oil. Season with salt and pepper. Roast in a 350 degree oven approximately 45 minutes, or until squash is tender enough to be pierced with a fork. Remove squash from the skin and pass flesh through a tamis or strainer. Season the puree with vinegar, salt and pepper. Fold in the butter.

3. For the Gremolata, mix all ingredients in a bowl, and season to taste.

4. To serve, divide squash evenly on 6 plates. Top with beef, then top beef with Gremolata.

Nestled in the back of the historic Farm at South Mountain, Quiessence has been a culinary oasis since 2004. The lush, green surroundings make the city feel far away (even though it's surprisingly close to city life), while chef Gregory LaPrad's contemporary American farm cuisine showcases Arizona's finest farmers, herdsmen and artisans on its daily-changing menu. As illustrated by this recipe, organic range-grazed Limousin beef—raised in Southeastern Arizona by the Power family—has consistently been a cornerstone of the Quiessence menu. "When thinking about ranching tradition in Arizona," LaPrad explains, "I thought it important to represent a beef dish served with simple-to-make seasonal complements, including apples that grow near Willcox where our beef is produced. It would pair beautifully with a wine from the region as well."

Recipe courtesy of
Quiessence Restaurant
*Chef Gregory LaPrad
Phoenix
602-276-0601*

ANCHIOTE PORK TENDERLOIN
WITH SMOKED APPLE CREAM, AU-GRATIN POTATO AND SAUTÉED SPINACH

Recipe courtesy of
Ranchos de los Caballeros
Chef Alex Kurtz
Wickenburg
928-684-5484

SERVES 6

1	pork tenderloin, about 3/4 pound
2 tablespoons	anchiote paste
1/2 teaspoon	olive oil
1 ounce	fresh squeezed orange juice

AU-GRATIN

1 cup	heavy cream
1 sprig	rosemary
2 cloves	garlic, minced
1	shallot minced
2	Idaho russet potato, peeled and thinly sliced
	Salt and pepper to taste
1/2 cup	shredded Manchego cheese
1 teaspoon	butter
1 tablespoon	shallot, chopped
1/2 tablespoon	garlic, chopped

SMOKED APPLE CREAM

1 cup	fresh apple juice
1	gala apple, peeled and diced
1/2 cup	heavy cream
1/2 tablespoon	olive oil
2 cups	spinach
	Salt and pepper to taste

1. To prepare the pork, clean all fat and silver skin from pork. In mixing bowl, combine achiote paste, olive oil and orange and whisk together until smooth. Rub onto pork and put in zip lock bag refrigerate 4 hours.

2. Preheat oven to 300 degrees. For the au gratin, add cream, rosemary, garlic, and shallots to saucepan and simmer on low heat until slightly thickened and reduced, about 10-12 minutes. Slice potatoes thinly and hold in water until cream is ready. When cream is reduced, strain and place in bowl with potatoes, Manchego, salt and pepper and toss. Pour into non stick casserole pan. Cover and bake at 300 degrees for 1 1/2 hours.

3. To prepare the smoked apple cream, heat sauté pan on medium high heat. Add butter, and when melted, add garlic and shallots and sauté about 5 minutes. Add apple juice and reduce by three-quarters. And 1/2 cup heavy cream and diced apple. Simmer, reducing by one-quarter. Blend sauce in food processor and add salt and pepper to taste.

4. Heat sauté pan on medium high heat. Add oil, and when hot, add spinach. Sauté 2-3 minutes or until spinach is wilted

5. To serve, top tenderloin with smoked apple sauce, spinach and au gratin potatoes.

After a round of 18 holes, stop into the spa for a Golfer's Relief Massage, and then sit back, relax and enjoy the decadent dining room at one of Arizona's oldest historic resorts—Ranchos de Los Caballeros. The ranch captivates guests with its Old West charm, but is anything from the typical "dude ranch." Meals are included in the price of your stay, including top-notch breakfasts, lunches and dinners, with every meal hand-crafted and inspired by Ranchos' talented culinary team.

GRILLED BUTTERNUT-TUSCAN KALE SALAD

SERVES 4

1	medium-large butternut squash
4 tablespoons	olive oil
2 - 3 tablespoons	red wine vinegar
1 tablespoon	honey
1 teaspoon	fresh rosemary, chopped
1 clove	garlic, sliced
	Salt and pepper to taste
1-2 bunches	Tuscan kale, sliced in ribbons
	Grilled squash
	Reserved dressing
3-4 ounces	sheep's milk feta or goat cheese, crumbled
4 tablespoons	Toasted pepitas or pecans

"Coming from a family of Italian immigrants who came to Arizona in the early '50s, I appreciate the sensibility, goodness and beauty that comes from hard work and self-reliance—good, honest labor that reflects and respects nature. I think that's what Arizona is all about, and that's the spirit I keep when I cook," says Chef Chrysa Robertson, who's been serving simple, comforting American cuisine at her stylish, Old West-inspired restaurant since 1993. An Arizona Culinary Hall of Fame "Chef Extraordinaire Award" winner and founder of Phoenix's first slow-food convivium, Robertson is all about sourcing local, seasonal ingredients. This hearty salad combines her favorite green with the savory sweetness of grilled winter squash.

1. Peel and de-seed squash, cut 1/2-inch thick slices. Whisk oil, vinegar, honey, rosemary and garlic. Season with salt and pepper.

2. Reserve half for salad dressing and toss remaining half with sliced squash. Marinate for 2-8 hours.

3. Season squash with salt and pepper, grill over coals until tender, turning frequently. Cool completely, cut into chunks.

4. Toss the butternut chunks with a bit of dressing, set aside. In bowl, toss sliced kale with dressing to taste. Divide kale on plates. Arrange squash, cheese and nuts on top. Serve.

Recipe courtesy of
Rancho Pinot
Chef Chrysa Robertson
Scottsdale
480-367-8030

RAZZ'S BOUILLABAISSE

Recipe courtesy of
Razz's Restaurant
Chef Erasmo Kamnitzer
Scottsdale
480-905-1308

Erasmo "Razz" Kamnitzer comes from a long lineage of restaurateurs and chefs and with Razz's Restaurant, he has fulfilled his heritage and passion for the culinary world. Razz, along with his wife Bobbi Jo Haynes, can be found hustling and bustling in an open kitchen, cooking dishes based in French technique, reflecting his South American and European roots. Last summer in Spain, he and his family enjoyed a serving of bouillabaisse. Back in his kitchen the scent bouillabaisse brewing reminds him of family, friends, gorgeous views and most of all, good food.

SERVES 4-6

6 tablespoons	olive oil, divided use
2	large carrots, cut into large chunks
4	stalks celery, cut into large chunks
1	medium onion, chopped
2 teaspoon	garlic, chopped
1/2 teaspoon	thyme, chopped
3	bay leaves
1/2 teaspoon	rosemary, chopped
1/2 teaspoon	parsley, chopped
1 quart	fish stock
1 quart	tomato juice
1 cup	white wine
1 teaspoon	chili paste
4	large shrimp
12	green mussels
4	large scallops
1	lobster (optional)
12	clams (cockles or manilas)
12	black mussels
8 ounces	firm fish (bass / tuna)
2	medium tomatoes, chopped

1. Heat two tablespoons of olive oil in a saucepan. Add carrots, celery and onions. Sauté until onions are transparent, about 5 minutes. Add thyme, bay leaves, rosemary, parsley and garlic; stir for 30 seconds and add white wine. Bring to a boil and add stock, tomato juice and chili paste. Cook until carrots are tender, about 5 minutes and set aside.

2. Heat 4 tablespoons of olive oil in large pot. Add shell fish and toss around. When clams, mussels start opening, add fish and tomatoes. Add broth with vegetables and cook for about 12 minutes to finish. Remove bay leaves before serving.

RED CHILI CHOWDER

SERVES 8-10

Recipe courtesy of
Rod's Steakhouse
*Lawrence and Stella
Sanchez, Owners
Williams
928-635-2671*

*Located on Historic
Route 66, Rod's Steakhouse
has been serving mouthwatering
slabs of barbecue ribs and
famous prime rib au jus for
more than 50 years. When
dining at Rod's, residents
of Williams and visitors
on their way to the Grand
Canyon, can appreciate
the home-style hospitality
of owners Lawrence and
Stella Sanchez, who can be
found in the restaurant daily.*

1 pound	pinto beans, soaked overnight
4 strips	bacon, chopped
	Salt to taste
	Black pepper to taste
1/4 teaspoon	garlic salt
1/4 teaspoon	white pepper
	Seasoning salt to taste
1/2 teaspoon	oregano
2 cubes	beef bouillon or 2 teaspoons beef granules
1 tablespoon	oil
1 pound	ground beef
1	large onion
2 cups	zucchini, chopped
6 cups	potatoes, cubed
8-10 teaspoons	all-purpose flour (depending on how thick you want the soup)
1 carton (about 16 ounces)	red chili puree
1 bag (about 10 ounces)	frozen whole kernel corn

1. Add the beans, bacon, salt, pepper, garlic salt, white pepper, seasoning salt, oregano and beef bouillon to a medium soup pot. Cook over medium heat until beans are tender, about 1 hour.

2. Meanwhile, in large frying pan, heat oil until hot. Sauté ground beef, onion, zucchini, and potatoes in oil until tender and lightly brown. Add flour, one teaspoon at a time, to the mixture to soak up oil and thicken soup. Add cooked beans and stock to meat mixture in frying pan. Mix well. Add red chili puree, corn and mix well. Simmer all ingredients together for approximately 20 minutes, or until heated through.

BUMBLEBERRY PIE

SERVES 4-6

1 cup	sugar
5 tablespoons	flour
2 tablespoons	cornstarch
1/2 teaspoon	cinnamon
1 1/2 cups	red raspberries
1 1/2 cups	blackberries
1 1/2 cups	Marion berries
1	pie crust for double-crusted pie (can substitute favorite pie crust recipes)
3 tablespoons	butter, sliced thin
1	egg

1. Preheat oven to 375 degrees. In a medium size bowl, mix together sugar, flour, cornstarch and cinnamon. Set aside.

2. In a large bowl combine berries. Sprinkle the sugar mixture on top the berries and gently toss. Place a single pastry sheet on the bottom of a pie pan. Add sweetened berries into your pastry. Place butter on top of the pie and top with second pastry. Place on top of pie, and seal by crimping the edge.

3. In a separate small bowl, beat egg until well and brush on top crust. Make a few slips in the crust to allow steam to escape.

4. Bake for about 35-40 minutes in the lower 1/3 of oven, or until pie is a deep, golden color. Cool pie before serving, top each slice with vanilla ice cream and serve.

Recipe courtesy of
The Rose Restaurant
Chef Billie Jo Nelson
Prescott
928-777-8308

Billie Jo Nelson, owner of The Rose Restaurant, bakes handmade pies every day at her restaurant, The Rose. Born and raised in Minnesota, Billie Jo, along with her husband Ron, owned a restaurant for 6 ½ years before moving to Prescott and purchasing The Rose. She believes that food should be as pleasing to the eye as to the palate—hearty yet elegant—and that texture and temperature must never be sacrificed for appearance or flavor…all add to the dining experience. All senses should be engaged: Sight, feel, taste, touch and even sound. Billie Jo invites you to The Rose for fine dining tradition in a 114-year old Victorian, vernacular cottage. Romance, warm service and exceptional food await you!

SONORAN SPINACH SALAD
WITH TEQUILA LIME

SERVES 4

Recipe courtesy of
**Screaming Banshee
Pizza and Wine Bar**
*Chef Ulysses Grant
Bisbee*
520-432-1300

Once a mining town, Bisbee has transformed into a haven for Bohemian lifestyle. Screaming Banshee Pizza and Wine Bar exudes that vibe, making it one of the most popular destinations in town. Converted from an old gas station, the space is best described as industrial-meets-Southwestern-grit. The owners have imbued the space with its warmth.

The house-made sauce, fresh mozzarella and hand-crafted, wood-charred crust make the pizza take on a life of its own with every bite. And it's not a bad place to grab a drink either, with fine cocktails and a wide selection of Arizona beers on tap.

2	ears of corn
	Olive oil for rubbing
1/4 cup	blanco tequila
1 3/4 cups	lime juice
1 teaspoon	salt
2 teaspoons	black pepper
2 tablespoons	oregano
3 cups	grape seed oil, plus a little more for rubbing
1 1/2 pounds	fresh spinach
2	jalapeños, seeds removed and diced
1 can (16 ounces)	black beans, rinsed and drained
2	fresh red bell peppers, seeds removed and diced

1. Shuck corn. Rub lightly with a little bit of oil. Broil or grill until corn is golden brown, about 15 minutes turning every 5 minutes. Let corn cool. Place one end of the ear in the bottom of a bowl and shave kernels off all sides.

2. In blender or food processor, add lime juice, tequila, salt and pepper and oregano. Turn on and start to drizzle in oil slowly until there is no more. Toss with washed spinach then place in a serving bowl or bowls.

3. Sprinkle remaining ingredients over top of salad.

GRILLED PORK TENDERLOIN, SMOKED TOMATO GRITS

SERVES 4

Recipe courtesy of
**Host of Check, Please!
PBS**
*Chef Robert McGrath
Scottsdale
602-264-2655*

Don't let the awe-shucks attitude and well-worn Stetson cowboy hat fool you; Robert McGrath is one of Arizona's finest chefs and restaurateurs. Winner of the prestigious James Beard "Best Chef in America: Southwest" Award, host of the Emmy Award winning show Check, Please!, founding chef of Roaring Fork and Renegade Canteen in Scottsdale, Arizona, McGrath has been a nationally noted chef for nearly two decades. McGrath's culinary career began with classical training in France before he navigated the plains and deserts of the Southwest, honing his craft and making a profound impact on the creation of Sourhwestern cuisine. McGrath has penned his own cookbook, American Western Cooking from the Roaring Fork, and was selected by Food & Wine magazine as one of the "Ten Best Chefs in America."

SAUCE

1/2 cup	coarsely cut bacon
1 quart	rich chicken broth
1	smoked ham hock
1 cup	demi-glaze

GRITS

1 cup	yellow Southern-style grits
1 1/2 cups	chicken stock
3/4 cup	smoked tomato puree
1/4 cup	dried jack cheese
1/4 cup	milk
	Kosher salt and cracked black pepper to taste

PORK

4	7-ounce pork tenderloins
2 tablespoons	bias-cut scallions
1 tablespoon	minced garlic
1/4 cup	oblique-cut red onion
1/4 cup	oblique-cut yellow squash
1/4 cup	cut baby bok choy
12	sprigs chervil
1 tablespoon	olive oil
	Kosher salt and cracked black pepper to taste

1. For the sauce, render the bacon then add the chicken stock and bring to a boil. Reduce in volume by half. Reduce the heat to a low boil, add the demi-glace and reduce the volume by half and strain. Cover and set aside in a warm place.

2. For the grits, bring the chicken stock to a boil, add the grits and reduce the heat to low. When the grits are cooked, fold in the smoked tomato puree, dried jack cheese and milk. Season to taste.

3. Season the pork and grill to the desired temperature. Glaze the pork as it comes off the grill. Sauté the onions and scallions in the olive oil until they are just tender. Add the bok choy and yellow squash. Season to taste. Place the vegetables in a small mound off-center on plate.

A pair of comfortable jeans or the latest fashions would feel appropriate at Spotted Donkey Cantina. The neo-Western atmosphere is stunning, with a luminescent wall of fiery red blocks, elegant lounge seating and rustic-yet-industrial nuances. James Beard Award-winning Chef Robert McGrath has taken classic Western cuisine and given it a modern-day edge with Green Chile Pork Stew, Oaxaca Mole Poblano, and Lobster and Corn Gravy.

CAULIFLOWER SOUP

Recipe courtesy of
St. Francis Restaurant
Chef Aaron Chamberlin
Phoenix
602-200-8111

SERVES 8

2 tablespoons	butter
2 cups	leeks, large chunks
2 cups	onion, yellow, large dice
1 tablespoon	salt
1	cauliflower head or 2 1/2 quarts cauliflower floret, roughly chopped
1/2 gallon	water
1 cup	cream
1 teaspoon	fresh thyme leaves picked
1 tablespoon	vinegar
2 dashes	Tabasco
	Salt to taste
	Cracked pepper to taste
	Capers, rehydrated raisins or chives for garnish

When you pair a chef trained by world-class talent like Jean-Georges Vongerichten with a raw, urban space, magic is bound to happen. St. Francis is just that. A modern, family-owned establishment with food as inspired as its architectural details, chef/owner Aaron Chamberlin has crafted a menu centered on the tools at his disposal, namely a wood-fired oven that cranks out everything from chorizo flatbreads to pork chili verde with homemade cornbread. Those conscious of their caloric intake will also rejoice, as Chamberlin has a number of healthful dishes in his repertoire, from roasted salmon with red quinoa and soy beans to a forbidden rice bowl topped with seven seasonal veggies.

1. Add butter to a deep sauté pan and heat on medium heat. When melted, add onions and leeks. Sauté until soft, about 5-7 minutes, and season with tablespoon of salt. Add cauliflower and water to cover. Add cream and thyme. Increase heat to high and bring to a boil. Reduce heat and simmer about 10 minutes, or until cauliflower can be pierced with a fork.

2. Puree and pass through a China cap or large mesh strainer. Add vinegar and Tabasco, and re-season with salt and pepper.

3. To serve, divide among bowls and garnish with capers, rehydrated raisins or chives.

BUFFALO MEATLOAF

Recipe courtesy of
The Stockyards Restaurant
Chef Michael Shea
Phoenix
602-273-7378

SERVES 4

1/2 cup	favorite barbecue sauce
1/4 cup	white onion, finely diced
1/4 cup	celery, finely diced
1/4 cup	carrot, finely diced
1 tablespoon	butter
1 pound	ground buffalo
1/2 pound	ground beef
1	large egg, beaten
3/4 cup	panko breadcrumbs
1	large clove garlic, minced
1 tablespoon	Dijon mustard
1 tablespoon	Worchestershire sauce
1 dash	Tabasco
1/2 teaspoon	salt
1/2 teaspoon	pepper
3 strips	raw bacon

1. Preheat oven to 350 degrees. Set aside 1/4 cup of barbecue sauce. In a large sauté pan on medium heat, add butter and, when melted, sauté onion, celery and carrots until tender, about 5-7 minutes. Cool slightly. Add vegetables and all ingredients, except bacon, in a large bowl and mix with an electric mixer or spoon until completely blended.

2. Spray a loaf pan with non-stick spray and bill with mixture. Pat down until firm.

3. Spread reserved barbecue sauce on top of the loaf, and sprinkle with black pepper. Lay the bacon strips lengthwise on top of the meatloaf. Bake uncovered in a 350 degree oven for about 1 hour. Let rest for 5 to 10 minutes before removing from the pan and serving.

Situated in the former administrative building for the Tovrea Land & Cattle Company, "Arizona's Original Steakhouse" opened its doors in 1947, serving up top-notch beef to the city's power brokers. Nowadays, the restaurant celebrates its heritage with updated, retro-chic Western decor and "New West cuisine" that merges Southwestern culture and culinary trends with indigenous ingredients. Chef Michael Shea says he chose this recipe for its connection to Arizona's past and present. "The buffalo was a staple for the Native Americans for centuries, and cattle is one of the Five C's; beef was a major part of Arizona's more recent history. This recipe combines both of those traditions."

HUEVOS RANCHERO

Recipe courtesy of
Sylvia's La Canasta
*Chefs Sylvia Menchaca
and Diane Hamel
Phoenix
602-269-2101
602-242-4252*

Sylvia's brings more than just Mexican food to the table. Culture is alive in every corner of the place. Walls are painted in dynamic turquoise, bright yellow, bold red and purple. Mexican mosaic tiles complete every table and energetic music plays in the background. The décor is welcoming and warm, just like the service and chefs. Stop in any day to one of Sylvia's two Phoenix locations and munch on many of your favorite Mexican classics.

SERVES 4

RANCHERO SAUCE

1	medium yellow onion cut in half and thinly sliced
1	fresh jalapeño, cut in half and thinly sliced
3-4	green onions, about 1/2 cup, cut 1/2 inch long
3 tablespoons	butter or margarine
3	medium red ripe tomatoes, sliced in thin rounds
2 cups	chicken broth
1 cup	water

SPICES

1/2 teaspoon	garlic
1/4 teaspoon	cumin
1 small pinch	oregano
1 tablespoon	fresh cilantro, minced
	Salt and pepper to taste
2 tablespoons	cornstarch, mixed with a little water

HUEVOS

8	fresh corn or flour tortillas
1/2 cup	oil
8	large eggs
1 cup	grated cheddar cheese
	Diced scallions for garnish

1. In medium skillet, heat butter or margarine on medium heat. When melted, add yellow onions, jalapeños and green onions. Cook vegetables until soft and pale in color. Add tomatoes and stir. Cover and simmer, stirring often until the mixture resembles tomato paste. Add chicken broth, water and spices. Increase heat to medium high, and simmer for an additional 10 minutes. Add fresh cilantro, reduce heat and simmer 10 minutes. Add cornstarch mixture, using discretion to thicken. Remove from heat and set aside.

2. Prepare a plate with paper towel lining to soak up oil from tortillas.

3. In medium skillet, heat half of the oil. Using tongs, dip tortilla into hot oil. Do not leave in the oil more than 2-4 seconds. Place lightly fried tortillas on the lined plate to absorb excess oil. As an alternate to frying, place tortillas between dampened paper towels and heat for 10 seconds in microwave.

4. Place two corn tortillas on each serving place before you start cooking eggs. Fry eggs to taste, either over-easy or sunny-side up. Place 2 cooked eggs atop lightly fried or softened corn or flour tortillas. Smother eggs and tortillas with the ranchero sauce. Sprinkle with grated cheese. Repeat until you have completed your plates. Garnish with finely chopped green onions.

MEDITERRANEAN PAELLA

Recipe courtesy of
T. Cook's at the Royal Palms Resort and Spa
Chef Lee Hillson
Phoenix
602-808-0766

SERVES 4

1	onion, diced
4 tablespoons	olive oil, divided
1 cup	white rice
2 cups	chicken stock
1 pinch	saffron
	Salt and pepper to taste
1	garlic clove, sliced
2 tablespoons	olive oil
6 ounces	Spanish chorizo
16	cockles
16	mussels
16	shrimp, 26-30 count
3/4 cup	diced pork
1/2 pound	chicken breast
1	red pepper, diced
2	tomatoes, diced
3/4 cup	chicken stock
1 sprig	thyme, leaves removed and stalk discarded
1 sprig	parsley, leaves removed and chopped
1/2 pound	butter
	Salt and pepper to taste

1. For rice, heat a saucepan on medium high heat. Add 2 tablespoons olive oil, and when hot, add onions and sauté for about 2 minutes. Add rice and stir continuously until the rice starts to slightly brown. Add the chicken stock, saffron and season with salt and pepper. Bring the liquid to a boil and then reduce the heat to a simmer according to package directions or until the rice has absorbed all of the liquid. Spread the rice out on a sheet pan and cool.

2. To make paella, heat saucepan on medium high heat. Add olive oil, and when hot add garlic. Sauté quickly, about 1-2 minutes, being careful not to burn. Add the chorizo, cockles, mussels, shrimp, pork and chicken in order in 15 second intervals, stirring between each addition. Add the tomato and red pepper, and continue to sauté for 2-3 minutes. Deglaze the pan with chicken stock and add the calamari and saffron rice. Mix well, combining all ingredients. Cook until completely warmed. Season with herbs, butter, salt and pepper. Drizzle with olive oil and serve.

Vaulted ceilings, twinkling candles and luxurious, earth-toned decor complement the Colonial Spanish architecture at award-winning T. Cook's, a romantic fine-dining destination at the Royal Palms Resort and Spa. Executive Chef Lee Hillson's Mediterranean-inspired menu includes fragrant paella infused with precious saffron and studded with chunks of meat and seafood. "Paella is a fantastic dish that is loaded with flavor," Hillson explains. "You can customize it to your own tastes and make it personal. It is a complete entrée, meaning you do not need to serve anything else with it."

TAR'S SCOTCH BEEF WITH RED WINE GRAVY

Recipe courtesy of
Tarbell's
Chef Mark Tarbell
Phoenix
602-955-8100

Photo: Paul Markow/Markow Southwest

"I pay respect to Arizona's history and to the flavors and techniques of the indigenous people. At its core there are solid Americana and northern Mediterranean values, and Tarbell's menu is anchored in that. And even when delving into what is considered comfort food, I've kept a lightness that I think is necessary and respectful to living in this climate."

SERVES 4-6

4 ounces	vegetable oil (about 1/2 cup)
1	cross rib or chuck roast (6-7 pounds)
	Salt and freshly ground pepper
2 stalks	celery
2	medium carrots
1	yellow onion
1 teaspoon	chopped garlic
3	Roma tomatoes
2 cups	red wine
1 quart	water
	Fresh herbs such as parsley, thyme and oregano

GRAVY

2 tablespoons	flour
2 tablespoons	melted butter
1 quart	beef stock, low-sodium if desired
1 quart	veal stock, low-sodium if desired
1/2 bottle	dry red wine
2 sprigs	fresh thyme
2 cloves	garlic, peeled and halved
1/2	yellow onion
	Salt and freshly ground pepper

1. Preheat oven to 350 degrees and season beef with salt and pepper. In a heavy-bottomed pan, heat vegetable oil. Sear seasoned beef on all sides until dark brown. Remove from heat to small roasting pan.

2. In the same heavy-bottomed pan, sauté all vegetables until light brown. Addred wine, bring to a boil, stirring and lightly scraping the browned bits from the beef until they dissolve into the sauce. Keep boiling and stirring until the sauce is reduced by half.

3. Add sauce to beef in small roasting pan. Then add water, herbs of your choice (or from the above list), and cover. Let cook for about 2 1/2 to 3 hours, or until fork tender.

4. To make the red wine gravy, in a small pan add butter. Once melted, add flour, and stir until flour is integrated. Cook until the raw flour taste is gone. Ad liquids, thyme, garlic, onion and simmer to reduce by half, then strain, discarding solids. Season with salt and pepper to taste. Serve Scotch Beef surrounded with sautéed, seasonal vegetables and mashed potatoes.

While Tarbell's dining room is certainly seductive, with its crisp white tablecloths, dim lighting and dramatic modern art, some of the best seats in the house are at the long, curved maple bar overlooking the exhibition kitchen at this popular Phoenix bistro, which is a Food + Wine *Best Restaurant winner and 16-year recipient of* Wine Spectator's *Award of Excellence. Locals and tourists alike flock here for Mediterranean-inspired contemporary American cuisine by Paris-trained chef Mark Tarbell (who's also a longtime wine columnist for* The Arizona Republic). *Here, he shares the recipe for one of his most famous crowd-pleasers. He adds, "Scotch Beef is one of those dishes that haunt you. I get cravings for it."*

Photo: Paul Markow/Markow Southwest

GREEN CHILI

Recipe courtesy of
Tee Pee Mexican Food
Arte Killeen, Owner
Phoenix
602-340-8787

If you've lived in the Valley long enough, you probably refer to this dark, comfortable neighborhood favorite (a stagecoach stop in a former life) as "Tee Pee Tap Room," which was its original name when brothers John and Bill Hurguy opened it in 1958. Two years later, the Hurguys sold the business to their accountant, Tony Duran, and his wife, Anna. It's been in the Duran family ever since and is now run by Tony and Anna's children and grandchildren—Art, Kathy, Jeff and Julianna Killeen. The restaurant's stone-walled entryway is lined with pictures of famous visitors— including George W. Bush— who've all come to try the soufflé-like chile relleno and the legendary Mary Lou.

SERVES 4

2 tablespoons	vegetable oil
1 1/2 pounds	cubed pork stew meat
2 tablespoons	all-purpose flour
1 can, 4.5 ounces	diced green chile peppers, drained
1/2 can, 3.5 ounce	chopped jalapeño peppers
1/2	medium onion, chopped
5 tablespoons	tomato sauce
3 1/2 cups	water
	Onion salt to taste
	Garlic salt to taste
	Salt and black pepper to taste
	Corn tortillas for serving

1. Heat oil in a large cast iron skillet over medium-high heat. Stir in cubed meat, and cook until nicely browned and cooked through, about 15 minutes. Remove skillet from heat, and allow to cool briefly.

2. Sprinkle flour over pork. With a wooden spoon, stir pork to coat, scraping the bottom of the skillet to loosen browned bits. Add chile peppers, jalapeños and onions. Stir in tomato sauce and water. Season to taste with onion salt, garlic salt, and salt and pepper.

3. Return skillet to medium heat. Bring to a simmer, cover, and cook 30 minutes, stirring occasionally. Remove cover, and cook 10 minutes more.

4. Divide pork chili into 4 bowls and serve with corn tortillas.

TEXAZ RED CHILI

SERVES 4

4 pounds	coarse ground beef brisket
1/3 teaspoon	salt
2 cups	diced onion
2 tablespoons	minced garlic
1/2 cup	Gebhardt's chili powder
1/2 tablespoon	paprika
1/2 tablespoon	whole oregano
1/2 tablespoon	whole toasted cumin
1/2 teaspoon	cayenne
1/2 teaspoon	Tabasco sauce
1 tablespoon	crushed red pepper flakes
1 3/4 cups	beer
2 1/2 cups	tomato sauce
1/4 tablespoon	corn flour (masa harina)

1. Soak all spices in beer for 30 minutes.
2. Brown meat with salt and then skim fat.
3. Add onion and garlic, then simmer for 30 minutes.
4. Add spices and tomato sauce, then simmer on very low heat for 3 hours.
5. Skim grease as necessary.
6. Add corn flour mixed with 1 cup of water and simmer for 15 minutes.

Recipe courtesy of
TEXAZ Grill
Chef Steve Freidkin
Phoenix
602-248-7827

Saunter into TEXAZ Grill, and your eyes are instantly besieged by Texas artifacts. Road signs, posters, concert flyers, taxidermy, license plates, canned chili signs and neon beer logos are just the tip of the iceberg. Steve Freidkin created the Texas-style restaurant in 1985, and although their signature chicken-fried steak was not on the original menu, it has become the restaurant's legendary contribution to the Arizona culinary scene. More than three-quarters of a million TEXAZ chicken-fried steaks have been served to date, and counting.

CIDER AND TEA BRINED PORK PORTERHOUSE
WITH ROASTED APPLESAUCE

Recipe courtesy of
Tinderbox Kitchen
Chef Scott Heinonen
Flagstaff
928-226-8400

Within the narrow confines of this 1920s building, in which punched-tin ceilings and modern photography peacefully coexist, Chef and co-owner Scott Heinonen serves up "American comfort food redefined," an apt phrase for dishes that seamlessly blend old school and new. The charming patio in back shares a wall with one of 14 remaining Basque handball courts in the United States, built by Isabelle and Jesus Garcia in 1926 for the Basque sheepherders who drove their flocks to Flagstaff every summer. Heinonen says this recipe perfectly expresses what Tinderbox is all about: classic comfort sparked with imagination.

SERVES 4

4	pork Porterhouse chops, about 10 ounces each
1 quart	apple cider
1/4 cup	Kosher salt
1/2 cup	maple syrup
1 tablespoon	pickling spice
4	Gala apples
1 teaspoon	cinnamon
1 teaspoon	kosher salt
2 tablespoons	sugar
6 teaspoons	water

1. Preheat oven to 375 degrees. Combine cider, salt, maple syrup, pickling spice and mix well. Place chops in brine and refrigerate for 4 hours.

2. Peel apples, core and cut into wedges. Toss with cinnamon, salt and sugar. Roast for 20 minutes at 375 degrees. Cool apples. Place in blender with water. Puree for 30 seconds. Chill.

3. Remove chops from brine. Reduce brine to syrup and put aside to use as glaze. Grill or pan-roast chops for approximately 4 minutes per side or desired doneness. Brush chops with glaze and serve with chilled applesauce. Serve with braised Brussels sprouts or braised cabbage with bacon.

1929 CHILI

Recipe courtesy of
**Tom's Tavern &
1929 Grill**
Chef Jason Choat
Phoenix
602-257-1688

For nine decades, Tom's Tavern has been a well-revered dining establishment in the heart of downtown Phoenix. Since 1929, back when Tom Higley converted the old city morgue and old pipe shop into a burger joint and gin mill, Tom's has been a city favorite. Today, as Arizona celebrates its centennial, Tom's is once again experiencing a renaissance to complement what's happening in downtown Phoenix. While Tom's is being refreshed and renewed, its new owners, the Bidwill Family, are intent on ensuring that the traditions, character and rich political history of the tavern— established by previous owners from Tom Higley to Michael Ratner—continue well into the future matched by first class food.

SERVES 4

4 pounds	beef (brisket is the preferred cut) diced to 1/2 inch cubes
12	red bell peppers
5	Anaheim peppers
16 ounces	black beans cooked
6	garlic cloves, peeled and crushed
5 tablespoons	dark chili powder
2 tablespoons	cumin ground and toasted
1 tablespoon	smoked paprika
2 teaspoon	oregano
1 cup	olive oil
2 cups	yellow onion, diced to 1/2 inch cubes
4 cups	beef stock
4 tablespoons	tomato paste
	Salt and pepper, to taste
	Shredded cheddar, diced onion, sour cream, chopped jalapenos for garnish

1. Coat chilies in olive oil and place in pre-heated broiler or grill to char outer skin. Turn chilies every couple of minutes to evenly char. Once chili skins are black and blistered place in a medium sized bowl and cover with plastic wrap. Set aside for 5-10 minutes. Hold chilies under running water and remove skins, seeds and stems. Place cleaned chilies in blender and puree.

2. Heat remaining oil in a large stock pot over high heat. Place cubed beef in the hot oil and sear all sides. Add diced yellow onion and continue to brown the beef and onion mixture. Once onions start to brown add chopped garlic, chili powder, cumin, paprika and oregano, stir to combine. Add pureed chilies and black beans

3. Add beef stock to chili and bring to a slow boil. Once chili is boiling, reduce heat and allow to simmer for 1 hour. Remove a piece of beef from chili and test for tenderness. If it is tender enough, it should be ready to fall apart, add tomato paste to chili and continue to simmer for 15 minutes or until desired thickness is reached.

4. Place chili in serving dish and present with cornbread muffins, garnishes and a salad.

TUSCAN KALE SALAD

Recipe courtesy of
True Food Kitchen
Chef Michael Stebner
Valleywide
602-774-3488

What happens when you pair one of the most successful restaurateurs of the 21st century, Sam Fox, with the soothsayer of health, Dr. Andrew Weil? True Food Kitchen, of course. The restaurant is a haven for relaxation; from the over-sized wooden lamp shades that complement the wood tables and floorboards, to the lush foliage that is used as a divider between dining areas. The nature of the fare can be a relief for guests, too, as every item is intended for healthy lifestyles. Executive Chef Michael Stebner has crafted a menu of globally inspired cuisine with an emphasis not only on nutrition, but on flavor as well.

SERVES 4

BREAD CRUMBS

1/2	Italian-style loaf of bread
2 tablespoons	extra-virgin olive oil

SALAD

	Juice of 1 lemon
3 to 4 tablespoons	extra-virgin olive oil
2	cloves garlic, mashed
	Salt and pepper, to taste
	Hot red-pepper flakes, to taste
4 to 6 cups	Italian black kale, loosely packed and midribs removed (also called dinosaur kale and available at high-end grocery stores)
2/3 cup	grated Pecorino Toscano cheese, or any other flavorful grating cheese such as Asiago or Parmigiano, divided use
1/2 cup	freshly made bread crumbs

1. To make bread crumbs, preheat oven to 300 degrees. Cut bread into cubes and scatter on a baking sheet in 1 layer. Bake 15 minutes, or until cubes feel dry on the outside but still moist inside. When cool, place bread in a food processor and pulse into fine crumbs. Set aside 1/2 cup firmly packed bread crumbs. Save any remaining for future use.

2. Heat the 2 tablespoons oil in a sauté pan over medium heat just until warm, not hot. Add reserved bread crumbs and stir to coat with oil. Cook, stirring constantly, until bread crumbs are evenly golden brown and crunchy, about 5 minutes. Remove from pan and allow to cool before tossing into salad.

3. For kale salad, whisk together lemon juice, olive oil, garlic, salt, pepper and a generous pinch of hot red-pepper flakes. Pour dressing over kale in serving bowl and toss well. Add 2/3 of the cheese and toss again. Let mixture sit for at least 5 minutes. Add bread crumbs, toss again, and top with remaining cheese.

CHURRO LAMB TACOS

Recipe courtesy of
**Turquoise Room
at La Posada**
*Chef John Sharpe
Winslow
928-289-2888*

Built by Fred Harvey, designed by architect Mary Jane Colter and opened on the Santa Fe Line in 1930, La Posada is the last of the great railroad hotels, a grand evocation of a Spanish hacienda considered to be Colter's masterpiece. Chef John Sharpe, who presides over the rustic Turquoise Room, has created a masterpiece within a masterpiece, sourcing local honey, goat cheese, herbs and vegetables, making virtually everything in-house and enlisting Hopi women to make the restaurant's signature piki bread. His churro-lamb tacos are a nod to both Navajo and Hispanic cultures.

SERVES 4

2 pounds	trimmed lean leg or shoulder meat
1 tablespoon	soy sauce
2 tablespoons	Worchestershire sauce
2 tablespoons	chopped fresh mint
2 tablespoon	chopped fresh sage
1 tablespoon	garlic salt
1 teaspoon	ground black pepper
1 teaspoon	coriander ground
1 teaspoon	cumin ground
1 teaspoon	cinnamon ground
1 teaspoon	ground ginger
2 tablespoons	extra virgin olive oil

SALSA

2 cups	vine ripe tomatoes cut into 1 inch dice
1 cup	fresh tomatillo
1 cup	finely diced red onion
1-2	Serrano chilies, seeds removed and chopped fine (adjust for hotness).
2 tablespoons	chopped fresh cilantro
2 tablespoons	chopped fresh mint
1 tablespoon	chopped fresh sage
1	clove finely chopped garlic
1 teaspoon	sea salt
	Juice of two Key limes or one large lime
1 tablespoon	seasoned rice vinegar
	A few grinds of black pepper
	A pack of at least 25 soft white corn tortillas

1. Trim the meat of all sinew and excess fat. Cut into 1-inch thick slices and place in a bowl. Mix the meat with the soy and Worchestershire sauce. In a separate bowl mix all the dry ingredients and chopped herbs together and rub into the lamb pieces. Add the olive oil and mix well. Cover and marinade for 24 hours in the refrigerator.

2. To make salsa, mix all ingredients together in a large bowl. Cover and refrigerate overnight.

3. Pre-heat your grill to 500 degrees. It is critical to char meat well. Lightly oil grill and grill meat about 3 minutes each side for medium well. Allow meat to rest 3 more minutes before cutting into slices. While meat is resting, warm tortillas on the grill.

4. Divide lamb evenly between tortillas and serve with salsa.

ROASTED POBLANO PEPPERS

STUFFED WITH CARAMELIZED SWEET POTATOES

Recipe courtesy of
Velvet Elvis Pizza
Chef Cecilia San Miguel
Patagonia
520-394-2102

Roasted Poblano Peppers is one of the most popular specials offered at this quirky pizza place. Because the kitchen make small quantities, customers call ahead to "reserve poblanos." It is an outstanding dish, the combination of flavors is complex and simply delicious and definitely with the Southwest soul: a little bit sweet, a little bit spicy with lots of gastronomical surprises.

SERVES 8

12	large oven roasted Roma tomatoes, skins removed
4	large oven roasted red bell peppers, skins and seeds removed
	Olive oil for coating
8	large poblano peppers
7	large sweet potatoes, peeled, diced 1/2 inch pieces
1/2 cup or 8 tablespoons	butter, melted
1/2 teaspoon	cinnamon powder
2 tablespoon	brown sugar
1/2 cup	dry pomegranate/cranberry
1/2 cup	golden raisins
4 tablespoons	olive oil
1	large yellow onion, chopped
6	garlic cloves crushed
	Pinch of dry habanero pepper
2 tablespoon	brown sugar
1 teaspoon	dry oregano leaves
1 teaspoon	dry thyme
1 can, 6-ounces	tomato paste
1 bunch	fresh cilantro, chopped and used as garnish
	Salt and pepper to taste
1/2 cup	toasted almonds for garnish

1. Preheat oven to 400 degrees. To roast tomatoes and peppers, apply a very thin coat of olive oil to the tomatoes and peppers. Place them on a baking sheet and cook until the skins are light brown, about 12-15 minutes. Remove from oven, let cool and remove the skins.

2. To roast poblanos, heat dry skillet on medium high heat. Cut peppers in half lengthwise and add peppers, skin side down, and cook until slightly charred, about 5-10 minutes, turning occasionally to promote even roasting. Roast in batches if necessary. Remove from skillet and place in a sealable bag for about 10 minutes. Remove; allow cooling slightly, and using a paper towel to carefully pull off charred skins.

3. Lower oven to 375 degrees. Peel and dice the sweet potatoes, place diced potatoes in a baking dish, and cover with foil. Bake for 20 minutes. Remove from the oven and gently mix the sweet potatoes with the melted butter, cinnamon and brown sugar. Continue baking for another 20 minutes, until soft but not soft enough to be mashed. Remove from the oven and mix in the dry fruit.

4. In a sauté pan, heat olive oil on medium heat. Add onion, garlic, habanero and sauté until onions are translucent, about 5-7 minutes. Set aside.

5. In a blender, puree roasted tomatoes and roasted peppers, tomato paste, dry herbs and onion mixture in small batches to prevent overcrowding, about 1 cup at a time. Pour in a saucepot, return to the stove and bring to a slow boil. Gently for 30 minutes, stirring occasionally. Salt and pepper to taste and add the fresh cilantro and set aside.

6. To prepare stuffed peppers, place poblanos on a large baking sheet. Ladle roasted pepper and tomato sauce evenly in a layer approximately 1- inch deep. Stuff each pepper with the sweet potato mixture and bake uncovered for about 15 minutes at 375 degrees. Garnish with fresh cilantro leaves and toasted almonds. To toast almonds, heat an ungreased skillet on medium heat. Add almonds and cook, stirring often, until golden or about 3-5 minutes.

Whole wheat crust, organic ingredients, vegetarian soups, homemade pickled asparagus, authentic chorizo, a juice bar and a velvet Elvis painting—that about sums up what Velvet Elvis Pizza has to offer. The very charming Velvet Elvis Pizza restaurant serves up an unlikely mix of kitschy Southwestern décor paired with rustic elegance and the pizzas are outstanding. The pies are crispy, fresh, thin-crusted, hand-spun and stone-fired. Guests should plan ahead for the Inca Quinoa Pizza, prepared with quinoa flour, julienned vegetables, creamy cheese sauce and baked in a deep iron skillet— this pie requires 24 hours' advanced notice.

RACK OF LAMB WITH SPICY BELL PEPPER JELLY

Recipe courtesy of
Vincent on Camelback
Chef Vincent Guerithault
Phoenix
602-224-0225

SERVES 8

8 racks	lamb, between 12-14 ounces each, trimmed of all fat
	Salt and pepper
8 sprigs	dried rosemary

SPICY BELL PEPPER JELLY

2	red bell peppers
2	green bell peppers
8	red Serrano chilies
2 cups	sugar

1. Make the bell pepper jelly first. Slice or julienne the peppers and chilies, but do not remove the seeds. Mix in the sugar and let the mixture sit overnight in the refrigerator. The following day, cook the mixture over low heat in a saucepan for between 10 and 15 minutes without adding any liquid. The peppers and chilies mixes with sugar will create their own liquid. Cool the jelly and serve at room temperature.

2. For the lamb, season the lamb with salt and pepper. Preheat grill on medium high heat over mesquite wood or coals. When hot, lightly oil grill and add lamb. Grill 3 minutes per side for rare, 6 minutes per side for medium and 9-10 minutes per side for well done. To serve, cut the lamb into chops and arrange on serving plates. Add a sprig of the dried rosemary. To dry, bake rosemary at 325 degrees for 20 minutes.

3. Set each sprig alight, blow out the flame immediately and serve the dish right away, serve bell pepper jelly to the side.

Chef Vincent Guerithault's unique hybrid cuisine—which combines the precision and flair of classical French cooking techniques with Southwestern ingredients such as chile, cilantro, corn, masa and jicama—made his namesake Camelback Road restaurant a fine-dining destination when it opened 25 years ago. Since then, the chef has branched out into catering, an on-site farmers market and a next-door bistro, while also garnering numerous awards along the way (including a James Beard Award and France's coveted Chevalier de l'Ordre du Merite Agricole). And all along, Guerithault's rack of lamb has been a signature dish, teaming bold, spicy regional flavors with the rich flavors of French cuisine.

BARBACOA

Recipe courtesy of
Vitamin T
Chef Aaron May
Phoenix
602-688-8168

It's impossible to pigeon-hole celebrity chef Aaron May, the brains behind the elegant cocktail lounge Mabel's on Main, the Southern-style comfort food at May's Counter in Tucson, the tongue-in-cheek evocation of a Midwestern bar at The Lodge or the down-home but sophisticated breakfast classics at Over Easy. But Vitamin T — his tiny, color-drenched space in CityScape, which devotes itself to the tacos, tortas, tamales and other street foods of Mexico City — is arguably his most winsome effort to date. "T" fans show up in droves for the juicy Sonoran hot dogs, fabulous open-face tamales and, of course, the soft tacos filled with standout barbacoa: beef brisket, rubbed with coffee and chile de arbol, then braised to melting tenderness.

SERVES 8

1 brisket	12 pound whole brisket

RUB

1 1/2 cup	coffee grounds
3 tablespoons	cinnamon
4 tablespoons	chili de arbol
4 tablespoons	salt

BRAISE

1 can, 28 ounces	diced tomato
1/2	yellow onion, diced
5	garlic cloves, peeled and diced
1 1/4 cups	lime juice
1 1/4 cups	red wine vinegar
1/2 cup	salt

1. Mix all ingredients for rub in a mixing bowl. Rub over brisket, coating all sides. Allow to sit overnight uncovered in the refrigerator.

2. To cook brisket, pre heat oven at 450 degrees. Heat grill on medium high heat. Lightly oil grates and when hot, add brisket and char on both sides. Remove. Add braising ingredients in a deep roasting pan. Add brisket and add enough water to cover three-quarters of the pan. Cover with foil and cook at 450 degree for 3 hours.

DUET OF LAMBS
WITH VEGETABLE TORTE

SERVES 8-12

Recipe courtesy of
Vogue Bistro
Chef Aurore de Beauduy
Surprise
623-544-9109

As its name suggests, Vogue Bistro is a glamorous experience of culinary expressions by Chef Aurore de Beauduy, amid striking decor and a fashion designer-inspired martini bar. Located in the thriving Marley Park community in Surprise, Vogue Bistro is trend-setting enough even for a supermodel. Trained in France, Chef Aurore brings years of cooking in the best kitchens of France and the U.S., where she developed a passion for using locally grown produce. This passion is reflected in her typical daily dishes like scallops with local arugula, baby beets, mint and turnip puree or a breast of duck with local bitter greens, tepary beans and apple cider reduction.

LAMB

4 racks	lamb (preferably Colorado origin)
1 tablespoon	Maille mustard
1/2 pound	ground lamb
1/2 pound	dry mission figs
4 sprigs	fresh mint
6 sprigs	fresh cilantro
	Salt to taste
	Pepper to taste

BECHAMEL SAUCE

5 tablespoons	butter
4 tablespoons	all purpose flour
1/2	onion
4 cups	milk
1 teaspoon	freshly grated nutmeg
	Salt, to taste

VEGETABLE TORTE

6	zucchini, sliced lengthwise
4	yellow squash, sliced lengthwise
6	Japanese eggplants, sliced lengthwise
5	red peppers, de-seeded and sliced lengthwise
1 tablespoon	Sherry vinegar
1 tablespoon	honey
4 pints	Beech mushrooms
8	Roma tomatoes
2 cloves	fresh garlic
4 twigs	thyme
2 sheets	puff pastry
1/2 cup	Asiago cheese
1/2 cup	Fontina cheese

1. For lamb, sear each rack on cast iron pan on high heat, brush with Maille mustard and allow to rest. Place ground lamb in a bowl and mix with sliced figs, chopped cilantro, chopped mint, salt and pepper. Generously apply the mixture to the rack of lamb. Roast lamb 20 minutes for medium rare and allow to rest. Set aside.

2. For béchamel sauce, heat butter on low heat in a saucepan. Add flour and stir until smooth consistency. Continue to cook until golden color, about 7 minutes. In separate pan add onion to milk and bring to a boil, then add to a butter-flour mixture while continuously whisking until smooth consistency achieved. Add salt, nutmeg and cook for 10 minutes. Remove the onion and set aside.

3. For vegetable torte, preheat oven to 300 degrees and outdoor grill to medium high heat. Slice all zucchini, squash, tomato and eggplant lengthwise in 1/8 inch pieces. Lightly oil grill and cook vegetables for about 1-2 minutes a side. Set aside. Marinate red pepper in 1 tablespoon sherry vinegar and 1 tablespoon of honey in a baking dish. Roast in the oven about 25 minutes at 300 degrees. Set aside.

4. Heat oven to 350 degrees. Meanwhile, heat olive oil on medium heat in a sauté pan. Add Beech mushrooms, garlic and thyme and sauté for about 4-5 minutes, or until mushrooms have softened. Remove from heat and allow vegetables to cool. Spray baking pan and place puff pastry in pan, overlapping sides with the pastry. Sprinkle Fontina cheese on the bottom and assemble layered terrine of vegetables in the following order: zucchini, squash, eggplant, Asiago cheese, Beech mushroom, béchamel, red peppers and tomato. Top with puff pastry and join with the bottom piece. Bake for 45 minutes at 350 degrees.

5. To serve, place desired lamb and vegetable torte on a plate.

FONDUE

Recipe courtesy of
Windsor
*Craig DeMarco and
Lauren Bailey, Proprietors
Phoenix*
602-279-1111

Tucked into its namesake historic Phoenix neighborhood, Windsor is a hip, local hangout with one of the best patios in town. The second offering from the minds that created the uber-cool wine bar Postino, owners Craig DeMarco and Lauren Bailey kept it simple: high-quality wine and beer on tap, a robust selection of prohibition-era cocktails and a kitchen that cranks out casual and familiar bar food with an upscale twist. Save some room for the homemade ice cream and nostalgic candy offered at Windsor's own next door ice cream parlor, Churn.

SERVES 8-10

1 liter	2 percent milk
1 cup	yellow onions, small diced
2 cloves	2 cloves garlic, rough chopped
1/2 teaspoon	teaspoon red pepper flakes
1/4 pound	pound butter
1/4 pound	all-purpose flour
3 cups	NYC cheddar cheese
1/2 cup	Collier's cheddar
1/2 cup	Parmesan Reggiano, grated
1 tablespoon	Dijon mustard
1/2 teaspoon	Kosher salt
3/8 cup	Bud Light
1-2	fresh baked pretzels, available at specialty stores and bakeries
3	smoked chorizo sausage links (preferably Schreiner's Sausage in Phoenix)

1. Place milk, onions, garlic and red pepper flakes in saucepan. Simmer for 15 minutes, and then strain through a straining cloth or chinois to remove seasonings.

2. In a separate saucepan on medium heat, melt butter and add flour. Use a wooden spoon and stir constantly until roux has texture of wet sand. Add seasoned hot milk to roux, 1 cup at a time, whisking well. Allow sauce to thicken before adding additional milk. Bring to a simmer and continue whisking.

3. Add half the cheeses to sauce and allow all cheese to melt, whisking constantly. Add the rest of cheese and whisk until it melts.

4. Add in mustard, salt and beer and whisk to incorporate.

5. Strain through a chinois into a bain marie pot filled with warm water, or any double boiler and return to heat.

6. Serve warm or, to keep warm, in a bain marie pot with hot water.

7. Slice apples and chorizo and arrange on a plate. Warm fresh pretzels in the oven and brush with unsalted butter and sprinkle with sea salt and slice.

BEEF WELLINGTON

SERVES 4

Recipe courtesy of
**Wright's
at The Biltmore**
*Chef Todd Sicolo
Phoenix
602-381-7632*

Wright's at The Biltmore is the signature, fine dining restaurant at the historic Arizona Biltmore resort, the 82-year-old Grand Dame of Arizona. Wright's expert chefs focus on turning classical dishes into contemporary ones. Highlighting timeless dishes with an innovative approach is the method behind their genius. Sink into a Lobster Thermidor or Rack of Lamb and admire their innovative and fresh décor inspired by the organic Frank Lloyd Wright style and namesake of the restaurant. Stunning pendant chandeliers composed of globes of varying sizes, soft leather benches, and glass panels framed in wrought iron draw the eyes up to the block and gold-leafed ceiling.

MUSHROOM DUXELLE

1/2 pound	button mushrooms, chopped
1/2 pound	crimini mushrooms, chopped
2 ounces	thyme, tied
4	garlic cloves, minced
2	shallots, minced
1/4 cup	cottonseed oil

BEEF WELLINGTON

4	beef tenderloins, about 6 ounces each
16 tablespoons	mushroom duxelle
8 ounces	lace or caul fat
4 cups	potato puree
4	puff pastry cut into 4-inch squares
1	egg, beaten
4	baby carrots
4	cipollini onions
4 tablespoons	veal demi glace (available in gourmet markets)
8 tablespoons	Hollandaise sauce (see recipe below)

POTATO PUREE

5	russet potatoes, peeled
1/2 stick	butter
1/4 cup	heavy cream
	Salt and pepper to taste

HOLLANDAISE

1/2 cup	white wine
1	shallot
1	garlic clove
10	peppercorns
1/2 teaspoon	thyme
2	egg yolks
1/4 cup	clarified butter
1/4 teaspoon	paprika
1/4 teaspoon	Tabasco sauce
	Salt to taste

1. To prepare the mushroom duxelle, add oil to sauté pan on medium heat. When hot, add remaining ingredients and sauté until moisture has evaporated from the mushrooms to prevent puff pastry from becoming soggy.

2. Preheat oven to 350 degrees. Top beef tenderloin with equal amounts of mushroom duxelle and wrap with lace fat. Place tenderloin on top of puff pastry and wrap, sealing ends to keep ingredients in. Brush exterior of puff pastry with beaten egg and season with salt and pepper. Place carrots and onions in foil and place in the oven with Wellingtons. Bake at 350 degrees until puff pastry is golden brown, about 20 minutes. Let it rest for a few minutes, and just before serving, cut in half to expose the meat. Remove vegetables and keep warm until serving.

3. To prepare the potato puree, boil potatoes in water until they are fork tender, about 15 minutes. Remove from water and drain. Pass potatoes through a ricer to make them smooth, and then blend in butter and cream. Season with salt and pepper to taste.

4. To prepare Hollandaise sauce, place white wine, bay leaf, peppercorn, garlic and thyme in small pot. Simmer on medium heat until almost dry. Deglaze pot with a splash of water and strain into mixing bowl. Let cool, then add egg yolks. Place egg mixture in a double boiler over medium high heat and whisk the egg yolks until reduced and smooth. Remove from heat and whisk in clarified butter. Season with salt, paprika and Tabasco.

5. Place potato puree on a plate, then the Wellington, and garnish with the carrots and cipollini. Finish with the veal demi and hollandaise sauce.

NORTHERN ARIZONA VINEYARDS

ALCANTARA VINEYARDS

Alcantara Vineyards is a dream venture created by owner Barbara Predmore. Barbara and her husband, Bob, started the vineyard to provide their family and partners the opportunity to work and develop a vineyard community and winery, making wines that are comparable to the best of California and Europe. Barbara had spent four years of research and diligence using the best consultants from the University of Arizona and UC Davis, as well as support from her family at the noted Martin-Weyrich Vineyards in Central California. Alcantara Vineyard is perched on 87 acres of sloping terrain off the Verde River and Oak Creek. The Tuscan Farmhouse serves as the tasting room, where they host the many friends and guests that visit from around the globe. Check out their "green" winery building when you visit. Explore their website at **www.alcantaravineyard.com**.

CADUCEUS CELLARS

Maynard James Keenan created this label for his northern Arizona vineyards, Merkin Vineyards. One day while sipping some fine wine on his patio in the hills of Jerome, Arizona, he realized that the climate in the area was similar to the climates where some of his favorite wines were produced. Why not grow a vineyard here? When asked about the type of wine he intended to grow, he answered, "My art and music has been described as 'thick, dense, rich, complex, engaging, emotional and spiritual,' by those who are fans. And an 'acquired taste' for those kind others who are not." He felt that Arizona aligned with this description and that they were a match made in heaven. "Surely these qualities will be reflected in the wine that Arizona will present to us". (Oh, did we forget to mention he is the lead singer for Tool)? His wines can be purchased at select retail outlets as well as their tasting room in Jerome. Also available online at **www.caduceus.org**.

JUNIPER WELL RANCH VINEYARDS

Juniper Well Ranch and Vineyards is located at the base of Granite Mountain in Skull Valley just minutes from Prescott. Their delicious handmade wines will delight you as you enjoy a glass on their Fiesta Patio or a bottle in a charming and private log cabin in front of a cozy fire. The high altitude vineyards boast Tempranillo, Petite Sirah, Cabernet Sauvignon and Sauvignon Blanc. **www.juniperwellranch.com**

OAK CREEK VINEYARDS

Deb Wahl, owner of Oak Creek Vineyards & Winery, has heard many times that "good wine grows on gentle slopes with a river nearby" which is why her vineyard is located near beautiful Sedona, across from Oak Creek. In the higher elevations of the property, they grow Syrah and Merlot and in the lower portion, they produce Zinfandel and Chardonnay. There is great sun exposure and currently they have approximately 4,000 plants on just over ten acres. They produce full-bodied flavorful reds and lean whites in small batches, giving individual attention to each barrel. Visit **www.oakcreekvineyards.ne**t to learn more!

JAVELINA LEAP VINEYARD & WINERY

Javelina Leap Vineyard & Winery is located just ten miles outside the scenic town of Sedona, adjacent to the green belt of lower Oak Creek, across from an Audubon bird sanctuary and state fish hatchery. The property was part of the historic ranches in a valley known as Page Springs for its abundance of natural springs. The estate vineyards are on the slopes of an ancient volcano. These soils lend intense characters of minerals, earth and fruit to the wines produced here. The owners and winemakers, Rod and Cynthia Snapp, welcome you to their newly remodeled tasting room that is fashioned after a turn-of-the-century Western saloon. Many accolades and media attention have been given to the wines they produce here. They ask that you share these handcrafted wines with your friends and loved ones. The tasting room is open daily from 11 a.m. to 5 p.m. For more information, visit **www.javelinaleapwinery.com**.

PLEASANT VALLEY WINERY

The winery makes good-tasting wines for people who like to enjoy wine. Since 2000, they have been making wine in Pleasant Valley (Young, Arizona), known for its beautiful vistas, cold mountain climate, rarefied air and pure crystal waters, Young is also the home of the historic Graham-Tewksbury Feud of 1886; the Pleasant Valley Range War was the bloodiest in American history. Head to Young for an enjoyable day or week. Call the winery before you leave and they will happily open up the Little Log Cabin Wine Shop for tasting and sales. Try our award-winning Honey Mead wine. They're looking forward to seeing you there.

GRANITE CREEK VINEYARDS

From a love of the land sprang a relationship with grapes that culminated in superb, award winning, living wines with no added sulfites. Granite Creek Vineyards was founded in 1974 when owners Kit and Robin Hoult planted grapevines and began the 36-year legacy of Arizona's first and only Certified Organic Vineyard. Dedicated to environmental stewardship, Granite Creek Vineyards is a scenic environment to enjoy the ambiance of the vineyard's rural roots. Relax with picnics and great live music on this historic 100-year-old Arizona farmstead that has been nurtured to become sips of the enduring pleasures of fine wine. To learn more visit **www.granitecreekvineyards.com.**

FREITAS VINEYARDS

Freitas Vineyards is hidden away on the outskirts of Cottonwood. It's a small vineyard, the dream of Ray Freitas. She planted the 3 1/2-acre vineyard, located near the Verde River, in 2000 and has been tending her vines since. Her mission is to produce fruit forward wines, well balanced in flavor, color and aroma in order to stimulate and enhance your wine tasting experience. Ray calls her Malvasia "sunlight in a bottle". Freitas Vineyard produces only estate grown wines, utilizing the European tradition. You can taste Ray's wines at Pillsbury Wine Co. NORTH in Old Town Cottonwood. For more information visit **www.freitasvineyard.com.**

PAGE SPRINGS CELLARS

At Page Springs Cellars the goal is to create delicious wines that express the unique character of the landscape. They trust that their wines and winemaking convey their philosophies concerning family, education and living life to the fullest. Owner and Winemaker Eric Glomski feels strongly that growing grapes, making wine and raising a glass is a cultural ritual that fosters friendship, brings together families and unites communities. "Good wine is not strictly the esoteric fare of nobility. Wine is for the people." Not only does Eric have a vineyard in northern Arizona, he owns two additional vineyards in Willcox, AZ, including Arizona Stronghold, a second venture with Maynard James Keenan. Eric's vision is at the forefront of bringing Arizona wines onto the national stage. Learn more about their wines and events at **www.pagespringscellars.com**.

SYCAMORE CANYON WINERY

Sycamore Canyon Winery is located on the banks of Oak Creek just south of Sedona. Their mission statement is to create the finest-quality wines available anywhere in the world. The location of the vineyard was chosen because of the perfect microclimate for growing grapes: plenty of sunshine, clean water and a cold breeze that comes down from the Mogollon Rim which cools the grapes off every evening. All of their custom wines can be sampled at the Art of Wine in Sedona at the Hyatt Piñon Pointe Shopping Center. They are open seven days a week. **www.artowine.com**

SAN DOMINIQUE

An Arizona original, San Dominique is nestled at 4,600 feet, in the hills south of the Verde Valley. Atop a hill, just off the freeway, you can't miss the winery and tasting room. Also passionate about garlic, you'll find garlic flavored "everything" here! San Dominique is home to Bill Staltari, cellarmaster and garlic purveyor. Winemaking has been a tradition in Bill Staltari's family, stemming back to Calabria, Italy, where his father, Joseph, learned the art from his father, who in turn was taught by his father and his father's father . . . through five generations. Be sure to visit Bill next time you're passing through. His website is **www.garlicparadise.com.**

BITTER CREEK WINERY

Jerome's newest wine venture is an avant-garde ambiance of artwork in a first-class gallery showing some of the area's finest artists, and the place to be for a wine tasting. The vintner invites you to experience all of his nouveau varieties while watching the panoramic view across the Verde Valley with Sedona's red rocks in the distance. You will encounter a grand selection of unique, special press and hard to locate varietals. Their vineyard has 52 different varieties from cuttings taken from exceptional vineyards in Europe and the U.S. They aim to please even the pickiest palate. Once you're here, you won't want to leave. Open daily from 11 a.m. to 6 p.m. For more information, visit **www.bittercreekwinery.com**.

PAINTED LADY VINEYARD

In Skull Valley, the Painted Lady Vineyard grows Gewurztraminer grapes organically, without the use of toxic chemicals. The one-acre vineyard, originally planted in 2006, was harvested for the first time on August 31, 2009. This was supplemented with Gewurztraminer grapes from southern Arizona to create the first totally Arizona grown Gewurztraminer wine, the Painted Lady Vineyard has offered. The farming life still has its surprises (some good, some not) but optimism runs high! In the meantime Eric Glomski of Page Springs Cellars, their winemaker, continues to perfect the Painted Lady Vineyard Gewurztraminer, fermenting all the sugar out of the wine creating a beautiful dry Alsace-type wine. To learn more, call at (928) 442-9831 and check out **www.paintedladyvineyard.com.**

BURNING TREE CELLARS

Burning Tree Cellars is the Brainchild of long time Verde Valley resident and wine geek, Corey Turnbull. Alongside friend and partner, Mitch Levy, Corey has been working to make this dream a reality for the last four years. Burning Tree specializes in small batch, meticulously maintained, boutique wines using the finest available fruit sources, quality oak, patience and a whole lot of love. Batches are kept small and wines are kept close the vest. They want to share the wines with those who seek them out. You will not find any of these wines in your local supermarket. The 2009 Lotus and the 2009 Dragon are available now while the 2010 Peasant is slated to be released in late 2011. These handcrafted wines are only available at the Arizona Stronghold Vineyards Tasting Room located in Old Town Cottonwood as well as the Page Springs Cellars Tasting Room located in Page Springs. Visit at **www.burningtreecellars.com.**

ARIZONA STRONGHOLD VINEYARDS

Eric Glomski and Maynard Keenan purchased the historic Dos Cabezas Vineyards in early 2007 and renamed the Willcox vines Arizona Stronghold Vineyards. They believe that the soils and climate at the vineyard stand up to the finest in the world, feeling strongly that their wines express, first and foremost Arizona, and secondarily the grapes and hands of the vignerons involved. Their desire is to bring Arizona to the national wine stage, promoting their wines as value and quality based. They believe that great wine doesn't have to be expensive; it doesn't have to be pretentious; and it shouldn't be hard to find. It just has to be great and it has to be made by people that care. The Stronghold vineyard is nearly planted out at 80 acres. They also recently acquired the Bonita Springs Vineyard adding another 40 acres of vines and another 120 acres for potential expansion. Their tasting room recently opened in Old Town Cottonwood. Visit their website at **www.azstronghold.com**.

DIONYSIAN CELLARS

Dionysian Cellars was founded in 2007 by owner and winemaker, Darin J. Evans, with one goal in mind: to produce ultra-premium wines. All wines are created in a Dionysian fashion with respect to each wine's unique personality. They produce Barbera, Chardonnay, Tempranillo, Syrah, Pinot Noir and Malbec and are adding new and exciting varietals every year. Darin and assistant winemaker, Scott Waltz, have been making estate wines for Freitas Vineyard since 2007 and are in the process of planting vineyards in Northern Arizona. You can find the wines only at Wine Cellar in Old Town Cottonwood and in very select restaurants around the state. More at **www.dionysiancellars.com**.

JEROME WINERY

Jerome Winery was built on the side of Cleopatra Hill between Prescott and Sedona in the historic town of Jerome, featuring over 30 uniquely handcrafted, individually distinct wines. The vintner's philosophy is to create wines that are enjoyable for the novice and the connoisseur alike. The owner learned the art of wine-making by training as an apprentice under master winemakers. Varieties include Pinot Grigio, Mourvedre, White Zinfandel, Syrah, Muscat, Zinfandel, Sparking Wine, Cabernet Franc, Cabernet Sauvignon,

15-year-old Port and others that are soon to be added. In addition to the Jerome Winery, they have 100 acres of vines planted in southeastern Arizona, the Dragoon Mountain Vineyards. Visit their website at **www.jeromewinery.com**.

CELLAR DWELLERS

Cellar Dwellers Wine Co. was started by childhood friends Chris Babin and John Scarbrough. With enthusiastic fervor, a love of winemaking and Arizona, Chris and John have set out to create great Arizona wines that are hip, fun and accessible to all wine lovers. The first label released was their Tarantula Hawk, a 2008 Zin. Although the 2009 Canvas blend has sold out, you can find the 2009 Tarantula Hawk for sale at locations around Northern Arizona and select locations in the valley. The 2010 Cicada, a Sangiovese Cabernet blend, will be released this winter. Find our more at **www. cdwineco.com**. Also check them out on Facebook.

SONOITA/ELGIN VINEYARDS

LIGHTNING RIDGE CELLARS

After their first trip to Tuscany, Ron and Ann Roncone decided the wine they'd make would be based on their Italian heritage. Lightning Ridge Cellars, a small family winery, was established in 2005. It represents years of personal endeavor from the ground up. The Old World style of wines they make are simply the wines they enjoy most. Their estate wines are proudly made from classic Italian varietals: Sangiovese, Nebbiolo, Montepulciano, Primitivo, Malvasia and Muscat Canelli. Located at 5,100 feet elevation, the vineyards enjoy long warm summers and cool nights to provide the perfect combination for rich, full-bodied wines. They welcome you to their Tuscan-themed winery and tasting room. Visit **www.lightningridgecellars.com**

RANCHO ROSSA VINEYARDS

Rancho Rossa Vineyards is one of the largest family-owned wineries in the Sonoita area. It specializes in ultra-premium varietal bottlings from their 22 acres of estate plantings, using only 100 percent estate-grown fruit in their wines, the only winery in the area to do so. Their first vines were planted in 2002 and their second vineyard was planted in 2003. Rancho Rossa will donate 10¢ to the American Cancer Society for every bottle of wine sold. Visit the website at **www.ranchorossa.com** to learn more.

WILHELM FAMILY VINEYARDS

In 2003, Kevin and Karyl Wilhelm bought 20 beautiful acres of rolling Sonoita-Elgin wine-growing land to begin their winemaking dream. Today Wilhelm Family Vineyard is planted with seven different varietals, including Cabernet Sauvignon, Syrah, Merlot, Cabernet Franc, Petite Verdot, Tempranillo and Albarino. Other Spanish and Rhone varietals are currently being explored. Along with their wines, the Wilhelms' 6,000 square foot winery is available for custom crush processing operations, barrel storage and small individual lot winemaking. Karyl, their resident winemaker, has completed studies at U.C. Davis in the Winemaking Certification program. She prefers time-honored winemaking styles with patient guidance to nature's best. Visit **www.WilhelmFamilyVineyards. com** for the most current information about tasting hours, wine selection, and winery facility availability. Meet the family, sample their wines, and perhaps even try your harvesting and winemaking skills at their facility.

DOS CABEZAS

Dos Cabezas WineWorks has been producing wines in Arizona since 1995. Their award-winning wines have been served at the White House. The winery was originally located on 80 acres near Willcox, Arizona. Just after the harvest of 2006, winemaker Todd Bostock purchased the winery with the help of his wife Kelly and his parents Frank and Paula. The winery was moved to Sonoita, close to the vineyard the family planted in Elgin in 2003 Pronghorn Vineyards. They have since opened a tasting room at the winery and look forward to seeing you there soon. Visit them at **www.doscabezaswinery.com**.

CALLAGHAN VINEYARDS

Located in the rolling oak-dotted hills of southeastern Arizona, at an elevation of 4,800 feet, Callaghan Vineyards produces rich, complex red and white wines from its 25-acre vineyard. Mediterranean and Spanish varietals Petit Verdot, Petite Sirah, Tempranillo, Mourvedre and Grenache are the basic building blocks for their red blends, while Viognier and Riesling are blended for the estate wine. They soon will also include Marsanne, Roussane and Malvasia Bianca. From their first vintage in 1991, their wines have received many accolades from the most respected wine writers/publications in the world. Visit them at **www.callaghanvineyards.com**.

KIEF-JOSHUA VINEYARDS

Kief-Joshua Vineyards is a small family business on 20 acres in beautiful Elgin. The first planting was in 2003 and currently they have about ten acres under vine, consisting of eight different varieties: Tempranillo, Mourvedre, Petit Verdot, Cabernet Franc, Zinfandel, Riesling, Semillon and Viognier. The winemaker, Kief Manning, pursued viticulture studies in Australia, where he earned both a graduate and undergraduate degree in Viticulture and Enology. He practices traditional winemaking methods of minimal interference, open fermentation and barrel aging. He has also been practicing biodynamic growing procedures in the vineyard since 2006. Kief-Joshua Vineyards is a winery defined by family, passion and enthusiasm, with a commitment to winemaking that will exceed expectations. **www.kj-vineyards.com**.

CANELO HILLS VINEYARD & WINERY

Canelo Hills Vineyard and Winery is a family-owned and operated winery established in 2003 by Tim and Joan Mueller. They specialize in small production wines made from 100 percent Arizona grapes, and their wine reflects the influence of the Sonoita Appellaion's high desert. Offerings range from crisp, dry whites to full-bodied, spicy reds made form varieties like Syrah and Tempranillo. Visitors to the winery receive personal attention in the "warehouse chic" atmosphere of their tasting room. Learn more about them on their website at **www.canelohillswinery.com** and be sure to check out their blog.

CHARRON VINEYARDS

Charron Vineyards is a small boutique winery producing hand-crafted Arizona wines. The winery's signature White Merlot is made from grapes that are hand picked from mature vines grown at an elevation of 4,023 feet. The long warm summer days, cool nights and Empire Mountain terroir sets their Merlot grapes apart. Milton and Susan Craig invite you to taste their wines while enjoying the spectacular views of the Santa Rita and Empire Mountains. They are located in Vail, 3/4 of a mile off scenic Highway 83 between Tucson and Sonoita. The tasting room is open Friday through Sunday 10 a.m. to 6 p.m. and weekdays by appointment. Visit their website for more information. **www.charronvineyards.com**.

SONOITA VINEYARDS

Dr. Gordon Dutt, owner and founder of Sonoita Vineyards, is a retired soil scientist from the University of Arizona. As part of a research project back in 1973, he established an experimental vineyard on the red, acidic clay of the Babacomari Ranch in Southern Arizona. The success of that vineyard and the quality of the wines from those grapes led to the planting of a commercial vineyard in 1979, the first in the Sonoita-Elgin area. Sonoita Vineyards' winery opened in 1983 with a first-vintage production of 300 gallons. Today Winemaker Fran Lightly is producing nearly 4,000 cases (9,500 gallons) per year from 10 different grape varieties including Colombard, Sauvignon Blanc, Pinot Noir, Syrah, Merlot and Cabernet Sauvignon. Over 90 percent of this production is sold through a beautiful and spacious tasting room, gift shop and special events facility with picturesque views of hillside vineyards, rolling grasslands and scenic mountain ranges. This facility is open daily (except major holidays) from 10 a.m. to 4 p.m. Visit **www.sonoitavineyards.com** for more info.

HOPS & VINES

Partners Megan Haller, Shannon Zouzoulas and Summer Cantu created Hops & Vines to fulfill their collective dream. On a shoestring, they've created a unified vision that is opening in early 2012. Megan has worked at Sonoita Vineyards as well as with Kent Callaghan of Callaghan Vineyards. Rounding out her education by experience, she's also worked with Chris Hamilton of Rancho Rossa and Ann Roncone of Lightning Ridge Cellars. Creatively they've started their vision from scratch and intend to serve top quality wines and craft beers in their tasting room on Hwy 82. Be sure to stop by and enjoy the great views overlooking the rolling hills of Sonoita. Find out more on Facebook or on their website at **www.azhopsandvines.com**.

VILLAGE OF ELGIN WINERY

The Village of Elgin Winery emphasizes terroir. They stomp the grapes, use natural yeasts, hand craft and use only new wood casks. The winery accents small-lot red, white and rosé wines ranging from single varietals such as Sauvignon Blanc, Cabernet Sauvignon and Sangiovese to traditional blended delights. Each wine is handcrafted by the winemakers/owners Gary and Kathy Reeves. The Village of Elgin Winery is home to the WORLD renowned Tombstone Red which has spawned three other wines including a seven-year-old Cabernet Sauvignon named Tombstone Gunslinger and two whites, Tombstone Rain and Tombstone Showdown. Their Dry Rosé was the Rosé category Best of Class at the Governor's Choice. Learn more at **www.elginwines.com**.

FOUR MONKEY WINES

Four Monkey Wines, one of Arizona's new wineries, produces quality wines at reasonable prices; the four wines retail for under $11/bottle. The winery produces the Playful Monkey, a Cabernet Sauvignon and a 2007 Governor's Choice Wine Competition Silver Medal Winner. The other three wines are the Sinful Monkey, the Naughty Monkey and the Cheeky Monkey— encompassing two reds and two whites, all representing individual personalities. For tastings visit the Village of Elgin Winery. Learn more at **www.fourmonkeywines.com**.

SIERRA BONITA

Located northwest of Willcox in a valley created by the Winchester, Pinoleno and Galiuro Mountains, Sierra Bonita's name was inspired by its location adjacent to the historic Sierra Bonita Ranch. Here the Smith family cultivates the vines and produces wonderful wines with only estate fruit. Their first vineyard was planted in 1997 with Cabernet Sauvignon, Sauvignon Blanc and Syrah. A second vineyard was planted gradually, devoted to Petite Syrah, Grenache Noir, Grenache Blanc, Mourvedre and Tannat. There are now 11 acres of vines in production. The rootstock and clones were carefully chosen for this climate and soil, no pesticides are used, and all the skins and cuttings go back into the vineyards to reinvigorate the vines. The 2009 Cab and a Syrah were just released. **www.sierrabonitavineyards.com**.

LAWRENCE DUNHAM VINEYARD

We create hand crafted wines that reflect the unique characteristics of southeastern Arizona. Our philosophy of winemaking is to select the perfect varietals and let nature do its magic with as little intervention as possible. We let the fruit speak for itself. Rhone-varietals flourish in the volcanic soils of our 5,000-foot elevation estate in the Chiricahua Mountain foothills. Add clean air, pure water, mountain breezes and four seasons and we have the key ingredients that make up our outstanding terroir. Visit this magical place and experience the unique wines of the Lawrence Dunham Vineyards. Go to **www.lawrencedunhamvineyards.com** or call 602-320-1485 to join the Chiricahua Circle or wine club, purchase our wines, arrange for a visit, or attend an upcoming event. Wine tasting is by appointment only.

FORT BOWIE VINEYARDS

Fort Bowie Vineyards & Orchard Products features the freshest and finest products. Currently the Orchards produce Pecans, Walnuts, Peaches and Cherries. A variety of nut products including specialty roasted Cinnamon Sugared Pecans, Salted and Roasted Pecans, Chocolate Pecan Clusters and Pecan Oil can be purchased at their store year round. The Vineyards produce a unique diversity of wines ranging from their famous Arizona Sweet Water, a sweet white dessert wine, to their Pecan Delight, a distinctive sparkling wine with the essence of pecans. Fort Bowie Vineyards recently introduced a new line of Chocolate Wine Sauces and Wine Truffles. Wine tasting is offered daily. Find out more at their website at **www.fortbowievineyards.net**.

KEELING SCHAEFER VINEYARDS

At 5,000 feet above sea level, the summer climate of warm, sunny days and cool, high desert nights combines with the unique rhyolite volcanic soils to create wine with special characteristics. We produce estate grown and bottled wine on our 21 acres of vineyards located on Rock Creek on the western slope of the Chiricahua Mountains in far southeastern Arizona. We live on the estate, a little wine ranch on the side of the mountain, a quiet place far from the city, where one's life plays out along with the wine season. The winery and vineyard are not open to the public, however, we do accept visitors by appointment. Our new tasting room in Historic Downtown Willcox is open Thursday through Sunday 11 a.m. to 5 p.m. 520-824-2500 or **www.keelingschaefervineyards.com**.

CIMARRON

In the shadow of the Chiricahua Mountains at 4,300 feet., lies the fertile Kansas Settlement farmland. Oregon pinot pioneer Dick Erath chose this unique site to plant his Cimarron Vineyard. Planting traditional grapes alongside unique varietals, Erath plans to create wines to please the most discerning palate while retaining Arizona's unique terroir. His first vintage was released through select Fox Restaurant locations and future releases will be available through the tasting room at Dos Cabezas WineWorks in Sonoita.

GOLDEN RULE VINEYARDS

Nestled near the northern tip of the Dragoon Mountains, Golden Rule Vineyards enjoys an exciting blend of quartz and limestone soils and excellent water resources in combination with a high desert climate that provides intense sunlight, warm days, cool evenings and nearly constant air flows. Owners Jim and Ruth Graham and vineyard manager Don Sobey are proud of our young wines and enjoy sharing them with our friends. We believe our abundantly flavored wines represent our distinct terroir and our passion for excellence both in the growing of our fruit and the making of our wines. Varietals currently in production include Zinfandel, Sangiovese and Shiraz. We eagerly anticipate future wines produced from our developing vineyard blocks that include Cabernet Sauvignon, Petite Sirah, Grenache, Mourvedre, Petit Verdot and Cabernet Franc. Visit our website at **www.goldenrulevineyards.com** to learn more about our wines and vineyard operation.

SOUTHEAST ARIZONA VINEYARDS

SAND-RECKONER

Located on the Willcox Bench at 4300 feet in elevation, Rob and Sarah Hammelman tend to Sand-Reckoner Vineyards. The vines, grown on rocky, sandy loam soil, contend with the elements to fully express Arizona's rugged high desert. Rob's winemaking endeavors have taken him to Australia and France, and his wines represent a synergy between New and Old World winemaking. Wines produced by this new venture include Malvasia Bianca, a Rosé based on Nebbiolo, and reds from Sangiovese, Syrah, Graciano and Petit Verdot. Tastings are offered at their Willcox winery location by appointment. **www.sand-reckoner.com**.

CARLSON CREEK

Carlson Creek Vineyard is dedicated to the production of fine wine from Arizona. We are family owned and operated. Although we are a young company, we are filled with a passion for the grape vine. The vineyard's elevation provides a perfect climate for growing wine grapes. Carlson Creek Vineyard staff hopes you will come and visit its new Willcox tasting room. Learn more at **www.carlsoncreek.com**.

CORONADO VINEYARDS

In the shadows of the Dos Cabezas Mountains Mark and Jacque Cook planted the first vines at their El Pinito Vineyard in spring 2005. The vineyard is named for its lone, majestic pine tree, all that remains of what once was a golf course. The vines flourished and Coronado Vineyards is now proud to introduce you to their award winning wines. Each wine is drafted to be a unique experience: sweet table wines and exciting blends; gold medal sparkling wine Dolce Veritas; and fine varietals including Syrah, Cabernet Sauvignon and Riesling. El Pinito vineyard and onsite Taste of Coronado Restaurant, offer a perfect setting to enjoy wine and appetizers with a few friends, or hold a large private event or wedding. Chef Zach Hoffman and his warm and inviting staff strive to make each special event one to remember. Experience all that Coronado Vineyards has to offer. **www.coronadovineyards.com**

Special Thanks to Arizona Vines and Wines and Christina Barrueta for the information featured in this section.

A SAMPLE OF FARMS AND FARMER'S MARKETS

FARMS

Apple Annie's Orchard
2081 W. Hardy Road
Willcox, AZ
520-384-2084

Aravaipa's Painted Cave Cattle Company
92945 East Aravaipa Road
Winkelman, AZ
520-882-5020

Avalon Organic Gardens
2074 Pendleton Drive
Tumacacori-Carmen, AZ
520-603-9932

Buckelew Farms
17000 West Ajo Highway
Tucson, AZ
520-822-2277

Carefree Farms
36412 North 7th Avenue
Phoenix, AZ
623-780-0806

Chicken Scratch Ranch
23517 South 182nd Street
Gilbert, AZ
480-516-6317

Chiracahua Pasture Raised Meats
7708 Kansas Settlement Road
Willcox, AZ
520-507-3436

Citrus Heights Farm
4301 East McKellips Road
Mesa, AZ
480-832-4949

Crazy Annie's Chicken Farm and Wild Goat Hacienda
10207 East Mojave Greenway Road, Palominas, AZ
520-366-0035

Crow's Dairy Farm
11300 South Dean Road
Buckeye, AZ
623-261-2752

Date Creek Ranch
P.O. Box 1484
Wickenburg, AZ
928-231-0704

Desert Roots Farm
4776 E. Horse Mesa Trl.
Queen Creek, AZ
602-751-0655

Double Check Ranch
4965 N. Camino Rio
Winkelman, AZ
520-357-6515

Duncan Family Farms
17203 W. Indian School Road
Goodyear, AZ
623-853-0568

JH Grass Fed Beef
P.O. Box 63
Cave Creek, AZ
602-769-4614

Joharra Dairy Farms LLC
14429 West Earley Road
Casa Grande, AZ
520-876-5522

Lucky Nickel Ranch
7361 South Linda Lou Road
Eloy, AZ
520-709-2877

Malone Meat & Poultry Co.
102 West 29th Street
Tucson, AZ
520-624-4431

Marley Cattle Co.
2001 East Colter Street
Phoenix, AZ
602-269-6081

Marley Farms
26601 South Val Vista Drive
Gilbert, AZ
480-895-8130

Maya's Farm
6106 South 32nd Street
Phoenix, AZ
480-236-7097

McClendon's Select
15888 North 77th Avenue
Peoria, AZ
623-979-5297

Mother Nature's Farm
1663 East Baseline Road
Gilbert, AZ
480-892-5874

Mountain Shadows Dairy
6625 North Sarival Road
Litchfield Park, AZ
623-935-6077

Nature's Way Farm
42 Kipper Street
Rio Rico, AZ
520-761-9878

Phillips Family Farm
2107 S. Chuichu Road
Casa Grande, AZ
520-450-0182

Pistachio Valley Farm
9922 E. Lompoc Avenue
Mesa, AZ

Saddle Mountain Dairy
30359 W. Old US Highway 80
Palo Verde, AZ
623-393-8439

**San Rafael Valley
Natural Beef**
P.O. Box 547
Patagonia, AZ
520-394-0031

Schnepf Farms
22601 East Cloud Road
Queen Creek, AZ
480-987-3100

Shamrock Farms
40034 W. Clayton Road
Maricopa, AZ
480-988-1452

Singh Farms
8900 E. Thomas Road
Loop 101 & E. Thomas Rd.
Scottsdale, AZ
480-225-7199

Southern Arizona
Grass Fed Beef
8200 E. Box Canyon Road
Green Valley, AZ 85622
520-471-9462

Stotz Dairy
30005 West Yuma Road
Buckeye, AZ
623-386-5989

Stronghold Beef
P.O. Box 882
Pearce, AZ 85625
520-826-0009

Sundance Farms
4809 West Bechtel Road
Coolidge, AZ
520-723-7711

Superstition Farm
3440 South Hawes Road
Mesa, AZ
602-432-6865

The Ranch at Fossil Creek
10379 W. Fossil Creek Road
Strawberry, AZ
928-476-5178

Tolmachoff Farms
5726 North 75th Avenue
Glendale, AZ
623-386-1301

Triple G Dairy
29115 West Broadway Road
Buckeye, AZ
623-386-4565

Two Wash Ranch, Dave Jordan
New River, AZ
623-238-8654
Known for eggs—chicken, duck,
goose, guinea and pea fowl—as well
as unique herbs and vegetables

Valley Farms
26598 S. Brookerson Rd
Willcox, AZ
520-384-2861

Van Rijin Dairy
20102 East Warner Road
Mesa, AZ
480-988-9364

You-Pick Farms and Orchards
Visit **www.pickyourown.org** for
a list of Arizona you-pick farms
and orchards.

FARMERS MARKETS

Ahwatukee Farmers' Market

Year round

4700 East Warner Road
Ahwatukee, AZ

Ahwatukee Community Swim
and Tennis Center parking lot

Every Sunday

8:00 a.m. to 11:30 a.m.

602-919-9094

farmersmarket@q.com

Bisbee Farmers' Market

April – November

Bisbee, AZ

Vista Park in Warren

Every Saturday morning from
April 30 – November 20th

Summer - 8:00 a.m. to 12:00 p.m.,
Fall - 9:00 a.m. to 1:00 p.m.

520-236-8409

bisbeefarmersmarket@gmail.com

Borgata of Scottsdale

November – April

6166 North Scottsdale Road
Scottsdale, AZ

Scottsdale Road between
McDonald & Lincoln

Every Friday

1:00 p.m. to 7:00 p.m.

480-585-8639

mmevents@juno.com

Broadway Village Farmers' Market

Year round

2926 E. Broadway Blvd.
Tucson, AZ 85716

SWC of Broadway and Country
Club, Friday's Farmers' Market
at Broadway Village

Every Friday

10:00 a.m. to 2:00 p.m.

Junehussey@msn.com

Carefree Farmers' Market

Year round

100 Easy Street, Carefree, AZ

Carefree Amphitheater (Corner
of Easy St. and HoHum Rd. at the
Gardens, off Tom Darlington Rd.)

Every Friday

9:00 a.m. to 11:30 a.m.

602-919-9094

farmersmarket@q.com

Casa Grande Farmers' Market

Year round

On 3rd St. West of Florence St.

Every Tuesday and Saturday

8:00 a.m. to 12:00 p.m.

520-836-8744

downtown@cgmailbox.com

Cavallieres Family Farmers' Market

Year round

Reata Pass

Every Sunday

10:00 a.m. to 3:00 p.m.

480-766-3202

Chandler Farmers' Market

Year round

3 South Arizona Avenue
Chandler, AZ

Dr. A.J. Chandler Park/West side
of AZ Ave in the Ramadas.

Every Thursday

3:00 p.m. to 7:00 p.m.

info@chandlerfarmersmarket.com

Chino Valley Market

June 2 - September 29

1667 South Hwy. 89
Chino Valley, AZ

BonnFire Grill Restaurant

Every Thursday

3:00 p.m. to 6:00 p.m.

928-713-1227

Community Food Bank Farmers' Market

Year round

3003 South Country Club
Tucson, AZ

Between Ajo & 36th Street
on Country Club

Every Tuesday

8:00 a.m. to 12:00 p.m.

520-622-0525 ext 220

rojeda@communityfoodbank.org

Concho Farmers' Market

May 14 – October 29

Corner of Hwy 61 & 180A
in Concho

Every Saturday

May – September -
8:00 a.m. to 12:00 p.m.,

During October -
9:00 a.m. to 12:00 p.m.

info@conchofarmersmarket.org

Cornville Farmers' Market

June – September

9950 East Cornville Road,
Cornville, AZ

Every Monday

4:30 p.m. to 7:00 p.m. (or dark)

928-649-3190

loishoo@cableone.net

Cottonwood Farmers' Market & Jamboree

July – September

791 N. Main Street
Cottonwood, AZ
Main St in Old Town
Historic District

Every Thursday

5:00 p.m. to 9:00 p.m.

928-639-3200

hallen@ci.cottonwood.az.us

Douglas Mercado Farmers' Market

May 7th – October 29th

10th St.
Douglas AZ

Raul Castro Park

Every Saturday

9:00 a.m. to 1:00 p.m.

520-234-1211

brissa@douglasmercado.com

El Pueblo Farmers' Market

Year round

SouthWest Corner of Irvington Road and South Sixth Avenue
Tucson, AZ

El Pueblo Park

Every Saturday

Summer - 8:00 a.m. to 11:00 a.m.

520-622-0525

srickard@communityfoodbank.org

Elfrida Farmers' Market

April – November

10566 Hwy 191
Elfrida, AZ

Every Friday

2:00 p.m. to 6:00 p.m.

520-378-2973

jkarra@cchci.org

Estrella Lakeside Market

October – May

10300 Estrella Parkway
Goodyear, AZ

South of Elliott

Third Saturday of the Month

10:00 a.m. to 2:00 p.m.

480-585-8639

mmevents@juno.com

Farmers' Market at Park Place

Year round

5870 E. Broadway Blvd.
Tucson, AZ

Park Place Mall, at the South Courtyard (near Bamboo Club Restaurant)

Every Tuesday

1:00 p.m. to 6:00 p.m.

520-603-8116

Farmers' Market at Superstition Farm

Year round

3440 South Hawes Rd.
Mesa, AZ

Superstition Farm

Every Thursday Night

4:30 p.m. - 7:30 p.m.

602-432-6865

SuperstitionFarmMarket@gmail.com

Farmers' Market at Tucson Mall

Year round

4500 N. Oracle Rd.
Tucson, AZ

Courtyard next to the Cheesecake Factory

Every Thursday

10:00 a.m. to 2:00 p.m.

520-603-8116

Farmers' Market in Downtown Yuma

December – March

Main Street, Yuma, AZ

Downtown

Every Tuesday

10:00 a.m. to 3:00 p.m.

928-343-1243

Flagstaff Community Market

May 29 – October 9th

Corner of Rt 66 and
N Sitgreaves St

City Hall West Parking Lot

Every Sunday

8:00 a.m. to 12:00 noon

928-774-7781

flagstaffmarket@gmail.com

Flagstaff Community Market

July 6 – Sept 14

2257 E Cedar Ave (corner of 4th St and Cedar)

St Pius Church Parking Lot

Every Wednesday

4:00 p.m. to 7:00 p.m.

928-774-7781

flagstaffmarket@gmail.com

Fountain Hills Nocturnal Farmer and Crafts Market

January – April

Verde Road
Fountain Hills, AZ

Every Thursday

2:00 p.m. to 6:00 p.m.

480-585-8639

mmevents@juno.com

Gilbert Farmers' Market

Year round

222 North Ash Street
Gilbert, AZ

Downtown Gilbert next to the Water Tower

Every Saturday

7:00 a.m. to 11:00 p.m.

gilbertfarmersmarket@gmail.com

Globe-Miami Farmers' Market

June 25 - October 1

150 N. Pine Street
Globe, AZ

Veteran's Memorial Park
at Globe City Hall

Every Saturday

8:00 a.m. to 12:00 noon

928-812-3208

pauljensenbuck@gmail.com

Green Valley Farmers' Market

Year round

101 South La Canada
Green Valley, AZ

Green Valley Mall

Every Wednesday

Spring/Summer: 8:30 a.m.
to 12:30 p.m. - Fall/Winter:
10:00 a.m. to 2:00 p.m.

520-490-3315

villagemarket@ymail.com

Jesse Owens Park Farmers' Market

April − October

400 S. Sarnoff Drive

South of Broadway on Sarnoff

Every Friday

9:00 a.m. to 1:00 p.m.

520-882-2157

rox@mayatea.com

K & B Farms

May − November

NW Corner I-17 and
Orme Dugas Road

6 miles N. of Cordes Jct., 18
miles S. of Camp Verde

Thursday thru Sunday

9:00 a.m. to 5:00 p.m.

928-202-7393

Marana Farmers' Market

12375 N. Heritage Park Drive
Marana, AZ

West of I-10. under the Marana
Farm Ramada at the Heritage
River Park. South of the
intersection of Tangerine Farms
Road and Heritage Park

Every Monday

March − October: 4:00 p.m. to
7:00 p.m. / November - April:
3:00 p.m. to 6:00 p.m.

520-682-3837

Maya's Farm at South Mountain

October − May

6106 S 32nd Street
Phoenix, AZ

32nd Street & Southern

Every Saturday

9:00 a.m. to 1:00 p.m.

The Farm at South Mountain

6106 S. 32nd Street
Phoenix, AZ

(just south of southern on the
west side of 32nd Street)

602-276-6360

info@thefarmatsouthmountain.com

Mesa Community Farmers' Market

Year round

260 N. Center St.
Mesa, AZ

On Center St. just South of
University Dr. at
Rendezvous Green

Every Friday

9:00 a.m. to 12:00 noon

602-290-5067

mookie007@whoever.com

Momma's Organic Market

September − April

9744 W. Northern Avenue

West of Loop 101 and Northern
Avenue

Third Saturday of every month.

9:00 a.m. to 2:00 p.m.

602-703-7154

info@mommasorganicmarket.com

Norterra Farmers' Market

October − May

2460 West Happy Valley Road

The Shops at Norterra

1st and 3rd Wednesday
of the Month

3:00 p.m. to 7:00 p.m.

480-585-8639

mmevents@juno.com

North Peoria Farmers' Market

October 8th - April 14th

11150 W. Beardsley Road

Linden Tree Nursery

9:00 a.m. to 2:00 p.m.

602-703-7154

info@mommasorganicmarket.com

Old Town Farmers' Market

Year round

Brown and 1st Street
(next to the Carraige House)

Scottsdale

8:00 a.m. to 1:00 p.m.

623-848-1234

deniselogan@yahoo.com

Oracle Farmers' Market

Year round

2805 N. Triangle L Ranch Rd
Oracle, AZ

Historic Triangle L Ranch

Every Saturday

9:00 a.m. to 12:00 noon

520-896-2123

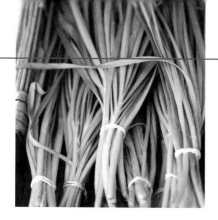

Oro Valley Farmers' Market

April – October

11000 N. La Canada Drive
Oro Valley, AZ

Southeast corner of La Canada
Blvd and Naranja Road

Every Saturday

8:00 a.m. to 12:00 noon

520-882-2157

rox@mayatea.com

Payson Farmers' Market

May – September

816 S. Beeline Hwy
Payson, AZ

Behind Chili's Restaurant

Every Saturday

8:00 a.m. to 12:00 noon

928-468-0961

PaysonFarmersMarket@gmail.com

Phoenix Public Market

Year round

14 E. Pierce / 721 N. Central

NE Corner of Central Avenue
& Pierce Street

Daily

Times vary

602-254-1799

cgentry@foodconnect.org

Pinetop-Lakeside Farmers' Market

May 11th – October 26th

1101 S. Woodland Road
Lakeside, AZ

At Mountain Meadow
Recreation Complex

Every Wednesday

2:30 p.m. to 6:30 p.m.

Info@Pinetop-LakesideFarmers-Market.org

Plaza Palomino Saturday Market

Year round

2970 N. Swan Road
Tucson, AZ

SE Corner of Swan
& Ft. Lowell

Every Saturday

9:00 a.m. to 1:00 p.m.

520-320-6344

Power Ranch at Trilogy Farmers' Market

October – April

4369 E Village Pkwy.
Gilbert, AZ

2nd Monday of the month

9:00 a.m. to 12:00 noon

480-585-8639

mmevents@juno.com

Prescott Farmers' Market

May 14th – October 29

1100 E. Sheldon St.
Prescott, AZ

Yavapai College main parking lot

Every Saturday

7:30 a.m. to 12:00 noon

928-713-1227

Prescott Valley Farmers' Market

June 1st – September 28th

Glassford Hiill & Park Avenue

Entertainment District Harkins
Theatre Parking Lot

Every Tuesday

3:00 p.m. to 6:00 p.m.

928-713-1227

Reese Family Farmers' Market

March – July

24712 S. Signal Butte Rd.,
Queen Creek, AZ

Signal Butte Road, just South of Cloud
Road. We are North of Riggs (also
Combs) and West of Rittenhouse.

Every Friday and Saturday

2:00 p.m. to 7:00 p.m. and 7:00
a.m. to 2:00 p.m.

Rincon Valley Farmers' Market

Year round

12500 E. Old Spanish Trail
Tucson, AZ

On Old Spanish Trail and the
Market will be in the big green
barn on the right.

Every Saturday

8:00 a.m. to 1:00 p.m.

520-591-2276

rvfm@rinconinstiture.org

Roadrunner Park Farmers' Market

Year round

3502 E. Cactus Rd.
Phoenix AZ

Between Freeway 51 & 36th St

Every Saturday

8:00 a.m. to 1:00 p.m.

602-290-5067

mookie007@whoever.com

Safford Farmers' Market

May – September

10th Ave & Thatcher Blvd

Parking lot of the Graham
County Chamber of Commerce
near Firth Park

Every Tuesday and Saturday

7:30 a.m. to 11:00 a.m.

928-428-6872

Saint David Farmers' Market

May 7th – October 29th

70 E Patton St.
Saint David, AZ

Solar Ramada near the Tennis
Courts at St David School

Every Saturday

9:00 a.m. to 12:00 noon

520-221-1074

stdavidfarmersmarket@yahoo.com

San Carlos Farmers' Market

May 5th – September 15th
700 Block of Laurel Street
Downtown San Carlos
Every Thursday Night
4:00 p.m. to 8:00 p.m.
650-802-4210
bmoura@cityofsancarlos.org

Santa Cruz River Farmers Market

May – September
100 S. Avenida del Convento,
Santa Cruz, AZ
West of I-10 at Congress and Grande
Every Thursday
4:00 p.m. to 7:00 p.m.
520-882-3304

Sedona Community Farmers' Market

May 26th - September 29th
3235 W. SR 89A
Sedona, AZ
Every Thursday
3:30 p.m. to 7:00 p.m.
928-821-1133
sedonamarket@gmail.com

Show Low Main Street Farmers' Market and Art Walk

May 14th – October 15th
Festival Marketplace in Historic Downtown Show Low
Between the Deuce of Clubs and East Cooley, between 9th and 11th streets
Every Saturday
9:00 a.m. to 1:00 p.m.
928-215-0451

Sierra Vista Farmers' Market

Year round
240 N. Hwy 90 Bypass (Saturday)
NW Corner of Carmichael & Wilcox (Thursday)
Every Thursday and Saturday
10:00 a.m. to 2:00 p.m.
520-678-2638
sierravistafarmersmarket@cox.net

Singh Farms

8900 E. Thomas Road
Loop 101 & E Thomas Rd
Scottsdale, AZ
Every Saturday
8:00 a.m. to 1:00 p.m.
480-225-7199
singhfarms@netscape.com
Known for their compost!

Sonoita Farmers' Market

June – September
Hwy 83
Sonoita, AZ
In front of Diamond JK Nursery and High Noon Feed Store
Every Saturday
9:00 a.m. to 12:00 noon
520-397-9269

St. Phillips Farmers' Market

April – October
4380 N. Campbell Ave.
Tucson, AZ
Southeast corner of River Road and Campbell Ave.
Every Sunday
8:00 a.m. to 12:00 p.m.
520-882-2157
rox@mayatea.com

Sunshine Herbs Farmers' Market

May 11th – October 5th
1020 E Huning Street
Show Low, AZ
Every Wednesday
9:00 a.m. to 1:00 p.m.
928-537-1711
sunshineherbs@hotmail.com

Tempe Farmers' Market

Year round
805 S. Farmer Ave.
Tempe, AZ
SE corner of Farmer & University
Daily
8:00 a.m. to 11:00 p.m.
Sunday - Thursday
8:00 a.m. to 11:00 p.m.
Friday 8:00 a.m. to 12:00 noon
Saturday 8:00 a.m. to 1:00 a.m.
480-557-9970
tempefarmersmarket@cox.net

The Camelback Market

October – May
3930 E. Camelback Rd
Phoenix, AZ
Adjacent to Vincent on Camelback
Every Saturday
9:00 a.m. to 1:00 p.m.
602-224-3727
leevon@vincentsoncamelback.com

Tonopah Rob's Vegetable Farm

Year round

35838 W. Buckeye Rd.
Tonopah, AZ

Every Saturday

623-386-3033

tonopahrob@gmail.com

Town and Country Farmers' Market

Year round

2021 E. Camelback Road,
Phoenix, AZ

20th Street and Camelback

Every Wednesday

10:00 a.m. to 2:00 p.m.

602-710-2122

lynn@tandcshops.com

Tuba City Farmers' Market

August – September

100 Aspen Drive
Tuba City, AZ

West side of St. Jude's Catholic
Church, in front of food bank

Every Wednesday

5:30 p.m. to 7:30 p.m.

928-283-6886

stjudefoodbank@frontiernet.net

Tubac Farmers' Market

October – May

Brasher complex of Plaza
De Anza

Every Thursday

10:00 a.m. to 2:00 p.m.

520-319-9868 x105

Twilight Farmers' Market at the Citadelle

June – September

19420 N. 59th Ave.
Glendale, AZ

59th Ave. and Utopia,
Arrowhead Ranch

Every Wednesday

5:00 p.m. to 8:00 p.m.

623-848-1234

info@arizonafarmersmarkets.com

Valley Of The Sun Farmers' Market

October 24th –
December 19th

12701 N. Scottsdale Rd
Scottsdale, AZ

Valley of the Sun Jewish
Community Center

Every Sunday

9:00 a.m. to 1:00 p.m.

623-848-1234

info@arizonafarmersmarkets.com

Verde Valley Farmers' Market

June – October

Main Street & Hollaman
Camp Verde, AZ

Ramada next to Ft. Verde
State Park

Every Saturday

8:00 a.m. to 12:00 noon

928-634-7077

Vistancia Country Club Farmers' Market

September – July

12902 W. Yellow Bird Lane
Peoria, AZ

4th Saturday of every month

10:00 a.m. to 2:00 p.m.

480-585-8639

mmevents@juno.com

Westgate Farmers' Market

October – May

6770 N. Sunset Blvd.
Glendale, AZ

Across from Cardinal's Stadium

2nd Saturday of the month

9:00 a.m. to 1:00 p.m.

480-585-8639

mmevents@juno.com

Wigwam Farmers' Market

May – September

300 East Wigwam Blvd.
Litchfield Park, AZ

Wigwam Golf Resort & Spa

Every Sunday

7:00 a.m. to 11:00 a.m.

623-935-3811

info@wigwamarizona.com

INDEX OF RECIPES

LIST OF RESTAURANTS

Amuse Bouche
17058 W. Bell Rd.
Surprise
623-322-8881

Asylum Restaurant
200 Hill St.
Jerome
928-639-3197

Atlas Bistro
2515 N. Scottsdale Rd.
Scottsdale
480-990-2433

Avanti
2728 E. Thomas Rd.
Phoenix
602-956-0900

Barrio Café
2814 N. 16th St.
Phoenix
602-636-0240

Beckett's Table
3717 E. Indian School Rd.
Phoenix
602-954-1700

Binkley's
6920 E. Cave Creek Rd.
Cave Creek
480-437-1072

Bobby Q's
8501 N. 27th Ave.
Phoenix
602-995-5982

Brix
16 N. San Francisco St,
Flagstaff
928-774-0541

**Bryan's Black
Mountain BBQ**
6130 E. Cave Creek Rd.
Cave Creek
480-575-7155

Café Poca Cosa
110 E. Pennington St.
Tucson
520-622-6400

Café Zu Zu
6850 E. Main St.
Scottsdale
480-421-7997

Canela Bistro
3252 Highway 82
Sonoita
520-455-5873

Carolina's Mexican Food
1202 E. Mohave St..
Phoenix
602-252-1503

Charlie Clark's Steak House
1701 E. White Mountain Blvd.
Pinetop
928-367-4900

**Christopher's & Crush
Lounge**
2502 E. Camelback Rd.
Phoenix
602-522-2344

Citizen Public House
7111 E. 5th Ave.
Scottsdale
480-398-4208

The Cottage Place
126 West Cottage Ave.
Flagstaff
928-774-8431

Cowboy Ciao
7133 E. Stetson Dr.
Scottsdale
480-946-3111

The Cowboy Club
241 N. Route 89 A
Sedona
928-282-4200

Dahl & DiLuca
7000 Hwy 179
Sedona
928-284-3010

Darbi's Café
235 E White Mountain Blvd.
Pinetop
928-367-6556

Diablo Burger
120 N. Leroux
Flagstaff
928-724-3274

Durant's
2611 N. Central Ave.
Phoenix
602-264-5967

Eddie's House
7042 E. Indian School Rd.
Phoenix
480-946-1622

El Charro Café
311 N. Court Ave.
Tucson
520-622-1922

EL Chorro
5550 E. Lincoln Dr.
Paradise Valley
480-948-5170

El Matador
125 E. Adams St.
Phoenix
602-254-7563

El Minuto Café
354 S. Main Ave.
Tucson
520-882-4145

El Molino Mexican Café
3554 N. Goldwater.
Scottsdale
480-946-4494

El Tovar
10 Albright Ave.
Grand Canyon
928-638-2631

elements
5700 E. McDonald Dr.
Paradise Valley
480-667-2300

Elote Café
771 Hwy 179
Sedona
928-203-0105

Essence Bakery
825 W. University Dr.
Tempe
480-966-2745

Feast
3719 E. Speedway
Tucson
520-326-9363

FnB
7133 E. Stetson Dr.
Scottsdale
480-425-9463

Gallo Blanco
401 W. Clarendon Ave.
Phoenix
602-274-4774

Garden Café
250 S. Madison Ave.
Yuma
928-783-1491

**The Garland's
Oak Creek Lodge**
8067 N. State Route 89A
Sedona
928-282-3343

Greekfest
1940 E. Camelback Rd.
Phoenix
602-265-2990

Heirloom
20775 N. Pima Rd.
Scottsdale
480-515-2575

House of Tricks
114 E. 7th St.
Tempe
480-968-1114

J&G Steakhouse
6000 East Camelback Road
Scottsdale
480-214-8000

Janos and J Bar
3770 E. Sunrise Dr.
Tucson
520-615-6100

Joe's Real BBQ
301 N. Gilbert Rd.
Gilbert
480-503-3805

**Josephine's Modern
American Bistro**
503 N. Humphrey St.
Flagstaff
928-779-3400

The Landmark
809 W. Main St.
Mesa
480-962-4652

La Perla Café
5912 W. Glendale Ave.
Glendale
623-939-7561

La Piñata
3330 N. 19th Ave, Phoenix
602-279-1763

L'Auberge Restaurant
301 L' Auberge Ln.
Sedona
928-282-1661

Leff-T's Steakhouse & Grill
150 S. Hwy 69
Dewey
928-632-1388

Lerua's Fine Mexican Foods
2005 E. Broadway Blvd.
Tucson
520-624-0322

Les Gourmettes
6610 N. Central Ave.
Phoenix
602-240-6767

Litchfield's at Wigwam
300 E, Wigwam Blvd.
Litchfield Park
623-935-3811

**Los Compadres
Mexican Restaurant**
4414 N. 7th Ave.
Phoenix
602-265-1162

Los Olivos Mexican Patio
7328 E. 2nd St.
Scottsdale
480-946-2256

Los Sombreros
2534 N. Scottsdale Rd.
Scottsdale
480-994-1799

Macayo's Mexican Kitchen
Valleywide
602-264-1831

Malee's on Main
7131 E. Main St.
Scottsdale
480-947-6042

Manuel's Mexican Food
Valleywide
602-957-7540

The Manzanita Restaurant
11425 E. Cornville
Cornvile
928-634-8851

Mastro's
Valleywide
818-598-5656

The Mission
3815 N. Brown Ave.
Scottsdale
480-636-5005

Molly Butler Lodge
109 Main St.
Greer
928-735-7226

Monti's La Casa Vieja
100 South Mill Ave.
Tempe
480-967-7594

**Mrs. White's
Golden Rule Café**
808 E. Jefferson St.
Phoenix
602-262-9256

Nobuo at Teeter House
622 E. Adams St.
Phoenix
602-254-0600

NOCA
3118 E. Camelback Rd.
Phoenix
602-956-6622

**The Original Garcia's
Las Avenidas**
2212 N. 35th Ave.
Phoenix
602-272-5584

**The Peacock Room
at Hassayampa Inn**
122 E. Gurle St.
Prescott
928-778-9434

Pepe's Taco Villa
2108 W.Camelback Rd.
Phoenix
602-242-0379

Petite Maison
7216 E. Shoeman Ln.
Scottsdale
480-941-6887

Pink Pony
3831 N. Scottsdale Rd.
Scottsdale
480-945-6697

Pinnacle Peak Patio
10426 E. Jomax Rd.
Scottsdale
480-585-1599

Pinon Bistro
1075 S. Highway 260
Cottonwood
928-649-0234

Pizzeria Bianco
623 E. Adams St.
Phoenix
602-258-8300

Posh Restaurant
7167 E. Rancho Vista Dr,
Scottsdale
480-663-7674

Quiessence
6106 S. 32nd St.
Phoenix
602-276-0601

Ranchos de Los Caballeros
1551 S. Vulture Mine Rd.
Wickenburg
928-684-5484

Rancho Pinot
6208 N. Scottsdale Rd.
Paradise Valley
480-367-8030

Razz's Restaurant
10315 N. Scottsdale Rd.
Scottsdale
480-905-1308

Rod's Steak House
301 East Route 66
Williams
928-635-2671

The Rose Restaurant
234 South Cortez St.
Prescott
928-777-8308

Screaming Banshee Pizza
200 Tombstone Cayon Rd.
Bisbee
520-432-1300

Robert McGrath
Host
Check, Please
602-264-2655

St. Francis Restaurant
111 E. Camelback Rd.
Phoenix
602-200-8111

The Stockyards
5009 E. Washington
Phoenix
602-273-7378

Sylvia's La Canasta
Valleywide
602-269-2101
602-242-4252

**T. Cook's at the Royal Palms
Resort and Spa**
5200 E. Camelback Rd.
Phoenix
602-808-0766

Tarbell's
3213 E. Camelback Rd.
Phoenix
602-955-8100

Tee Pee Mexican Food
602 E. Lincoln St.
Phoenix
602-340-8787

TEXAZ Grill
6003 N. 16th St.
Phoenix
602-248-7827

Tinderbox Kitchen
34 S. San Francisco St.
Flagstaff
928-226-8400

Tom's Tavern & 1929 Grill
2 North Central Avenue
Phoenix
602-257-1688

True Food
2502 E. Camelback Rd.
Phoenix
602-774-3488

**Turquoise Room at La
Posoda**
303 E. Second St.
(Route 66)
Winslow
928-289-2888

Velvet Elvis Pizza
292 Naugle Ave.
Patagonia
520-394-2102

Vincent on Camelback
3930 E. Camelback Rd.
Phoenix
602-224-0225

Vitamin T
1 East Washington St.
Phoenix
602-688-8168

Vogue Bistro
15411 W. Waddell
Surprise
623-544-9109

Windsor
5223 N. Central Ave.
Phoenix
602-279-1111

**Wright's at Arizona
Biltmore**
2400 E. Missouri Ave.
Phoenix
602-381-7632

CITRUS

CLIMATE

CULINARY